D0615454

Lost Fathers

Lost Fathers

The Politics of Fatherlessness in America

Edited by Cynthia R. Daniels

St. Martin's Press
New York

"Life Without Father" by David Popenoe reprinted and abridged with the permission of the author and The Free Press, a Division of Simon and Schuster, from *Life
Without Father: Compelling New Evidence that Fatherhood and Marriage Are Indispensable for the Good of Children and Society* by David Popenoe. Copyright © 1996
by David Popenoe.

Portions of "Growing Up Without a Father" by Sara McLanahan are reprinted with
permission from "The Consequences of Single Motherhood" by Sara McLanahan,
The American Prospect 18, Summer 1994, copyright 1994, The American Prospect,
P.O. Box 383080, Cambridge, MA 02138. All rights reserved.

"The Lost Children," by Jean Bethke Elshtain, first published in *The New Republic,*
Oct. 21, 1996. Reprinted by permission of The New Republic and Jean Bethke
Elshtain.

ISBN 0-312-21107-4

Library of Congress Cataloging-in-Publication Data
Lost fathers : the politics of fatherlessness in America / edited by Cynthia
R. Daniels.
     p. cm.
     Includes bibliographical references (p.) and index.
     ISBN 0-312-21107-4
Fatherless family—United States.   2. Paternal deprivation-
  -United States.   3.Afro-American fathers—United States.
   4. Absentee fathers—United States.   I. Daniels, Cynthia R.
HQ756.L67   1998
306.874'2—dc21   97-48633
                                                    CIP

First edition: June, 1998
10 9 8 7 6 5 4 3 2 1

for Katherine and Julia

Contents

ACKNOWLEDGMENTS

This collection grew out of a conference sponsored by the Center for the Critical Analysis of Contemporary Culture at Rutgers University in May of 1996. For their great help and support, I would like to thank those who participated in that event and in the yearlong inspiring seminar, "The Culture and Politics of Reproduction," which preceded it. Thanks to: Carolyn Williams, Leela Fernandes, Atina Grossman, Ynestra King, Adriana Ortiz-Ortega, Kathy Edin, John Gillis, Caridad Souza, Ruthie Gilmore, Carol Helstosky, Nicky Isaacson, Vincent Lankewish, Loretta Sernekos, Barbara Balliet, Elaine Chang, Sue Cobble, Drucilla Cornell, Judy Gerson, Janet Golden, Radha Hegde, Meredith Turshen, Roz Petchesky, Jacqui Alexander, Emily Martin, Donna Haraway, Lynn Randolph, Linda Gordon, Hortense Spillars, George Levine, Link Larsen, and Vanessa Ignacio. For their affectionate support, thanks also go to Bob Higgins, Katie Daniels, and Julia Daniels.

Lost Fathers

INTRODUCTION

Cynthia R. Daniels

FEW ISSUES IN THE 1990s generate such heat as the question of
fatherlessness. While public attention in the past decade has
focused relentlessly on single motherhood, the social and political
lens has now begun to shift to the place of *father* in the lives and
homes of women and children.

Controversy over fatherlessness has emerged at the center of
debates over welfare, poverty, sexuality, divorce, family values, and
"racial disorder." Yet it seems as if those engaged in debate—whether
in legislatures, policy circles or living rooms—can hardly agree on
the most fundamental terms of debate: Are there, in fact, more
children living without fathers today? Do children need fathers? Is
there a relation between fatherlessness and rising rates of crime and
destitution, or does father talk serve as mere subterfuge for more
fundamental discussions of poverty and inequality? What, after all,
is a father? It is not at all clear whether we should grieve the loss or
celebrate the transformation of contemporary fatherhood.

This collection presents the voices of a highly diverse group of
scholars to reflect on the culturally and politically charged concept of fatherlessness. Brought together, they illustrate the deep
and dramatic divisions that constitute public debate on this issue.
Debates over the proper or desirable place of fathers in the lives of
children revive old areas of controversy and initiate new ones.
Woven throughout exchanges over fatherlessness, for instance,
are questions regarding the nature of mothering and fathering, the
biological roots of sexuality and parenting, the relationship

between family structure and poverty, and the efficacy and desirability of alternative family structures. What I would like to do here is briefly preview some of the most fundamental points of controversy that run throughout the contributions to this collection. First: *What is fatherlessness?* Are fathers indeed more absent from the lives of children today? Second: *Does fatherlessness matter?* What are the consequences, for men, women, children, and society as a whole, of father absence? Third: *What is a father?* Can mothers, partners, brothers, uncles, adoptive fathers, or stepfathers fulfill the same functions as biological dads? The answers to these related questions hold profound implications for public culture, policy, and law.

WHAT IS FATHERLESSNESS?

Rising divorce and out-of-wedlock childbirth rates seem to suggest incontrovertibly that more children than ever are growing up without their fathers. Young women give birth and remain unmarried at unprecedented rates; middle-age women choose to become mothers without the support of male partners; marital unions dissolve under emotional or financial strain; husbands abandon wives and children with no looking back. Those most concerned with men's absence from the home point to all of these faces of fatherlessness in the contemporary American scene. Conservative scholars and critics argue that, while generated by a range of social pressures, fatherlessness results in the same devastating consequences for children: life without the emotional, moral, or economic support of father. In this collection, for instance, David Popenoe argues that the decline of fatherhood is one of the most unprecedented and devastating developments of modern time. And Maggie Gallagher argues that never before have we witnessed so profound and massive an abandonment of marriage—the only reliable vehicle we have to turn men into fathers and tie fathers to their children.

Yet others argue that the picture is far from bleak and far more complex. Historian Robert Griswold suggests that fathers have been absent from the lives of children before—drawn away from home by the pressures of industrial or agricultural work; by the demands of governing or war-making; or by cultural prescriptions that defined child nurturance as the province of women. And Judith Stacey argues that we are witnessing not a new and devastating decline in the quality of family life but a transformation of family structure where women are able to free themselves and their children from abusive or neglectful husbands and where the fathers who remain behind are involved in newer and richer ways with their children. Many argue that while divorce and out-of-wedlock childbirth rates reflect a profound level of change, they tell us little about the quantity or quality of the time men have spent, or now spend, with their children and even less about the ability of mothers alone (married or unmarried) to raise happy and healthy children.

In addition, arguments about the nature of contemporary fatherlessness as a new phenomenon have generated controversy over questions of racial and cultural diversity. For instance, both Dorothy Roberts and Lisa Dodson argue in this collection that, particularly in African American communities, "out-of-wedlock" does not always mean "without a father." Fathers may very well participate in families even when mothers remain unmarried. Roberts specifically argues that a multiplicity of family forms—including those headed by single mothers—have served well to raise African American children even under the harshest social circumstances.

Yet despite arguments regarding both historical precedent and cultural diversity, it is clear that family structures have changed dramatically over the past thirty years and that this change now persists across racial, class, and ethnic lines. For better or worse, for whatever its meaning, more than half of all children will now spend *some* time living without a father.

DOES FATHERLESSNESS MATTER?

What are the consequences of father absence for children and social structures? Across the political spectrum, talk about father-lessness has generated concern about both the social decay and costs to children of the absence of fathers from home. In this collection, for instance, David Popenoe argues that the absence of a strong paternal presence at home is the primary force behind the most disturbing problems that plague American society: crime and delinquency; premature sexuality and out-of-wedlock births; poor educational achievement; addiction and alienation among adolescents, and poverty for women and children. Like author Maggie Gallagher, he argues that men unconstrained by the bonds of marriage are more likely to produce lawless children and be lawless themselves. National movements to reunite fathers with children have assailed child custody laws, which purportedly produce estranged fathers, and have rallied against no-fault divorce.

While David Popenoe and other conservative scholars have focused on the social costs of fatherlessness, many others argue that the most severe costs of fatherlessness are suffered by children. Jean Elshtain, Sara McLanahan, and Maggie Gallagher all argue that there is convincing evidence that fatherless children live in poorer health, in worse home environments, and do more poorly in school than children with fathers present. Gallagher in particular focuses on the emotional impact of father loss. While academic and elite cultures blithely applaud and embrace "family diversity," she argues, children suffer grief, loss, and emotional hunger for unreachable fathers. Efforts to pluralize and liberalize marriage and divorce law consequently contribute to paternal abandonment at the children's expense.

In sharp contrast to these arguments, Judith Stacey decries what she perceives as perhaps a more dangerous trend than fatherlessness itself and that is the virtual social hysteria over the *idea* of father absence. Stacey argues that conservatives have simply shifted their judgmental focus from maternal to paternal laments, waging a national campaign to reinstate fathers at the expense of mothers and children. Such advocates have greatly exaggerated both the extent of father absence and the harm done to children by growing up in fatherless families. Presenting a vastly different view of the literature on father absence and harm to children, Stacey argues that efforts to measure social and emotional damage to children fail to adequately account for complex questions of causality (does poverty or father-lessness produce poor health?) and collapse important distinctions between different kinds of fatherless families.

WHAT IS A FATHER?

Debates over fatherlessness also have reinvigorated long-standing controversies over the biological roots of parenting and the sexual division of labor. Conservative scholars argue that models of "androgynous parenting" violate the most basic laws of sociobiology and that children have essential needs for both "mother love" and "father love." Many argue, for instance, that children have a founda-tional need for the two distinct kinds of love (and discipline) that the natural order provides and that the maternal/paternal balance is essential to the health and well-being of children.

Yet perhaps children don't need fathers at all, others argue, as long as they have access to at least one stable and loving parent of any sex. Or perhaps the functions traditionally performed by fathers might be performed quite well by mothers, aunts, grandparents, uncles, part-ners, or friends. Feminist scholars have defended both single-mother families and multiple family forms as alternatives to traditional nuclear relations. Presenting the voices of single mothers—who are all too often absent from debates over fatherlessness—Lisa Dodson sounds a cautionary alarm about the focus on father absence as one more way in which we implicitly condemn the job single mothers are now doing raising children. Unlike popular portrayals, she argues, many women who raise children without fathers exhibit extraordinary strength, resiliency, and independence of spirit.

Drucilla Cornell presents a more dramatic point of view, arguing that we must affirm "paraparenting" relations, where long-term parenting obligations are separate from often unstable sexual unions. Children may thus gain the commitment of many "voluntary" parents—women or men alone or in multiple partnership with others—who can provide a more secure foundation for their long-term love and care. Current distress over the disorder produced by fatherlessness and desires to constrain men through traditional heterosexual marital bonds are based, she argues, on false assumptions about men as naturally irresponsible and aggressive beings who must be tamed by women, custom, and law. In contrast, Cornell argues that father absence is produced by economic insecurity and oppressive standards of masculinity.

Regardless of one's position on any of these questions, it is clear that a great deal is at stake in debates over fatherlessness. Debates rage over marital and divorce law (Should we affirm or prohibit gay marriage? Should we tighten or ease restrictions on divorce?); welfare and poverty policy (Should we better support or withdraw resources for single mothers?); racial equality (Should we affirm or condemn cultural diversity in family form?); and reproductive law (Should we allow single women the right of access to sperm banks and technologies of reproduction?). All of these touch on and are touched by debates over fatherlessness. In the end, this collection aims to generate both more heat and more light on such questions and in doing so, it is hoped, move us closer to possible solutions.

STRUCTURE

Robert Griswold opens this collection with "The History and Politics of Fatherlessness." Griswold explores how changing conceptions of fatherhood over time have shaped and reshaped debates between liberals and conservatives regarding father time with children and the cultural place and moral worth of homes headed by women. Exploring in detail the political, cultural, and bioevolutionary assumptions of those at both ends of the political spectrum, he offers a historically grounded perspective on father absence in contemporary American homes.

David Popenoe's "Life Without Father" argues that the decline of fatherhood is one of the most basic and extraordinary social trends of our time. By the turn of the century, he projects, nearly 50 percent of American children may be going to sleep each evening without being able to say good night to their dads. He argues that we must restore marriage and reinstate fathers in the lives of their children if we are to reverse the serious social consequences of father absence.

In "Dada-ism in the 1990s: Getting Past Baby Talk about Fatherlessness," Judith Stacey analyzes national campaigns for "family values" during the 1990s that have shifted their focus from maternal to paternal laments. These crusades, which bemoan the socially corrosive effects of "fatherlessness," have issued forth from diverse sites across the political spectrum and now increasingly influence political response to family change. She criticizes the logic, data, and politics of the paternalist backlash but also argues for taking seriously the crisis of working-class masculinities that fuel the popularity of "dada-ist" fashions. Efforts to toughen divorce laws and reduce public support for single mothers are far more destructive to the health of children, she argues, than the absence of those fathers who disappear and who may in fact be neglectful or destructive of children's health. The solution is not to tighten the reins on single mothers and "milkbox dads" but to provide public support for a plurality of family forms and for all those who wish to be responsible and loving parents.

Sara McLanahan's "Growing Up Without a Father" analyzes the consequences for children of growing up apart from their biological fathers through divorce, adoption, separation, or non-marital birth. Through national longitudinal statistics, McLanahan explores how fatherless children fare in adolescence and young adulthood, including whether they give birth in their teens, finish high school, attend college, graduate from college, and find a steady job. She argues that parental breakup reduces children's access to important economic, parental, and community resources and that this trend holds true for children of different races, ethnic groups, and social classes. The remedy, she argues, requires tougher enforcement of child support obligations and the provision of universal programs for child care, health care, and income security for both two-parent and single-parent families.

Lisa Dodson presents a portrait of the challenging and rich lives of low-income single mothers in "'This River Runs Deep': Father Myths and Single Mothers in Poor America." She argues that the current focus on father absence as the most singular cause of emotional and economic distress for women and children diverts us from the true sources of poverty and ill-being and stigmatizes single mothers in the process. While most women and their children affirm the importance of fathers, and in fact often long for them, across racial and ethnic lines they affirm the deeper need to offset the relentless hardships that face all mothers, fathers, and children in low-income America.

Jean Elshtain, in "The Lost Children," returns us to questions of childhood harm in her analysis of teen single mothering. The United States has the highest rate of unwed teenage childbearing in the industrial world, and the best available evidence, she argues, demonstrates that teen parenting—which usually means parenting without a father—has heavy costs for children. Despite this evidence, feminist scholars continue to defend single teen parenting as a positive adaptation to adverse circumstances—promoting a cycle of irresponsible behavior that increasingly places young children at risk. This evasion often is due to feminist fears of feeding into the conservative hysteria targeting single mothers as the cause of all social ills. Yet this failure to address the harsh reality of what it means for young women (or girls) to parent alone helps to perpetuate the conditions which devastate families and children. Elshtain addresses these issues through a close examination of one recent and prominent feminist work, Kristen Luker's *Dubious Conceptions*.

In "The Absent Black Father," Dorothy Roberts considers the ways in which race influences our understanding of fatherlessness. She explores racial differences in the reasons for and policies addressing the absence of fathers as a symptom of rebellious Black motherhood. She further explores the forces that simultaneously disparage Black men and work to discourage their family participation. Welfare policy, joblessness, and the high rate of incarceration all contribute to Black fathers' absence from the home. While critics of Black fathers focus on marriage statistics, she argues that little attention is paid to the actual involvement of Black men in the lives of their children. These very critics do not seem to believe that Black fathers can serve as positive role models nor to care that most cannot provide adequate financial support for their children. New welfare policies that penalize poor Black women for failing to marry only worsen their families' welfare. In light of these contradictions, Roberts concludes that concerns about Black fatherlessness serve far more to discipline Black men and women than to improve the lives of Black children.

In "Father Hunger," Maggie Gallagher presents analysis of the losses suffered by children from paternal abandonment. She argues that the decline of fatherhood, both as a fact and a norm, is an unprecedented phenomenon. As many as half of American children experience not just fatherlessness but father abandonment—the knowledge that living fathers (who often may be nearby with new families) will not care for them. From the point of view of academics, this may be a story of personal freedom and tolerance;

from the point of view of children; it is often a story of unrequited love for unreachable fathers.

Drucilla Cornell's "Fatherhood and Its Discontents: Men, Patriarchy, and Freedom" takes on the growing movement in the United States that declares fatherlessness to be the cause of all social ills. The solution to crime, unemployment, government debt, female and child poverty, it is argued, is to return fathers to their proper place as heads of households. Cornell believes that this argument is fallacious, for it is based on assumptions that men are naturally "irresponsible, slovenly, murderously aggressive, rapacious, and polygamous" beasts who must be constrained by the humanizing effects of women in families. Contrary to such characterizations, father absence is produced not by the loosening of social constraints on men but by economic insecurity and unemployment coupled with the pressures of repressive standards of manhood. The solution lies not in reinforcing nuclear heterosexual norms but in accepting multiple family forms and paraparenting arrangements based on relations of true equality and mutuality between men and women.

Whether describing fathers lost to the shifts of the postmodern political economy or fathers lost through desertion or divorce, the voices presented here reflect the profound transformation of fatherhood being experienced by us all. It is to the nature and meaning of this transformation that we now turn.

ONE

THE HISTORY AND POLITICS
OF FATHERLESSNESS

Robert L. Griswold

DURING THE SUMMER OF 1996, the Promise Keepers filled football stadiums throughout the United States with thousands of men who sang, prayed, and dedicated themselves to renewing their Christian faith and their commitment to their families. Founded by former Colorado football coach Bill McCartney, the organization hopes to bring men to Christ while restoring their place as "spiritually pure leaders" both within their communities and within their homes. Promise Keepers urges that men—in fact, demands that men—back away from what one of the movement's leaders called "sissified self-indulgence and neglect" and reassume leadership of wives and children. Nor are these conservative Christians the only citizens concerned about fatherhood. For years the well-established Fatherhood Project in New York City has conducted research on fatherhood and held seminars on improving fathering, and in the summer of 1994 Vice-President Al Gore sponsored a conference on fathers and family life.[1]

Recently public and scholarly attention has focused on fatherlessness. Newspaper and magazine articles and a variety of critics from both the left and the right have added their voices to the debate, and two new books, David Blankenhorn's *Fatherless America* and David Popenoe's *Life without Father,* offer provocative, conservative interpretations of the purported crisis of "fatherlessness" in American society.[2] Not surprisingly, the left and the right share little common ground on this issue. Critics on the left tend to be more sanguine about the emergence of new family structures. Some see fatherless families as an inevitable by-product of a culture dedicated to personal freedom and female autonomy; others insist that fatherless families are often safer places for children than ones characterized by male domination and violence. Almost all on the left argue that single women, given adequate resources, are perfectly capable of rearing happy, healthy children and that families without fathers are simply one variant among many in the continuing evolution of family forms.

Conservatives reject such optimism. To them, many of America's most intractable problems, ranging from crime to poverty, teen pregnancy, and homelessness, can be traced to fatherlessness. Absent fathers have put American children at risk, and to forestall such problems, conservatives call for a return of fatherly authority, extol the virtues of traditional masculinity, and see in marriage and fatherhood a way to stem men's proclivity for sexual promiscuity and social disorder. What is needed, they argue, is a rebuilding process that will restore fatherhood to a central, vital place in our culture and in so doing end the "me-first egotism" that has created the current debacle.

Implicit in both views is a sense of what fatherhood once was and how it has changed over time. Conservatives and liberal feminists agree that for most of American history men had a secure place within their families, but the meaning they attach to this security is quite different. Those on the right celebrate traditional fatherhood and see within it a deep source of social stability and morality. Fathers once knew what was expected of them and passed the lessons of manhood to their progeny. Being a father had a certain "taken-for-grantedness" about it: A man did not have to be overly self-conscious about his responsibilities to be "good enough." His place in society had coherence, he was certain of who he was, and most important, he was a daily presence in the lives of his children.[3] As the head of his family, he played a vital role in building civil society. Now all is in ruin as men increasingly turn their backs on family commitments.

Where conservatives see declension, liberals often see progress. For some, the demise of the father is part of the slow erosion of male dominance, a sign that increasing numbers of women have the money and the gumption to make it on their own. In addition, the behavior of men who fail to support their children or, worse, never acknowledge them only confirms deep-seated suspicions about men in general. Many feminists celebrate the emergence of families headed by women and ask the wider culture to embrace this new variant as a step toward the liberation of women from male domination. Despite their appreciation for the financial difficulties of female-headed families and their well-placed contempt for men who neglect their children, the historical vision of these feminists is generally less pessimistic. Fatherless families should be seen as a viable alternative to traditional family life that deserves support—moral and economic—and not condemnation. It has taken a long time, they argue, to weaken patriarchal power, and nothing good can possibly come from movements hoping to restore male domination.

On one level, there is nothing the historian can do to settle this debate; it turns on deeply held ideas of the good society grounded in fundamentally different perspectives about gender and family. At another level, however, the historian can at least clarify the past, challenge the assumptions of both parties, and add another level of complexity to the discourse. That is the intent of this chapter. Reasons of space prohibit an exhaustive look at the subject, but a brief look at the historical evolution of fatherhood in America helps provide context for the contemporary debate about fatherlessness.

DEEP ROOTS

Today's concern about fatherlessness presupposes that life was different between fathers and children in the past. Specifically, most interpreters assume three things about past fatherhood: first, fathers and children more than likely lived together; second, fathers spent time with their children and played an important role in shaping their offsprings' development; third, fatherhood was ideologically coherent. Each supposition seems reasonable, but whether any is true is a complicated historical question.

The first point seems incontrovertible. Bioevolutionary evidence and the historical record both suggest that father-child coresidence has deep biological and social roots. The bioevolutionary perspective is important because it suggests just how fundamental the father-child bond is and how and why it developed over the long course of human evolution. While historians are understandably uneasy with any perspective that even hints at essentialism or genetic determination, bioevolutionary theory should not be ignored. In explicating the genetic meaning of paternal-filial bonds, it clarifies the significance of the cultural endorsement of marriage and fatherhood for men in the past and why the attenuation of father-child ties today is so significant.

At the core of the bioevolutionary perspective is an argument about the role of fatherhood in maximizing what evolutionary theorists call "inclusive fitness," that is, "the sum of an individual's own reproductive fitness together with his or her influence on the fitness of relatives."[4] For women, maximizing inclusive fitness means having children who survive, and the surest way to ensure survival lies in finding a mate who, after impregnation and birth, provides support and protection for mother and child. This "capturing of male energy into the nurturance of young," as two leading evolutionary anthropologists explain, may be "the keystone in the foundation of the human family."[5] In short, maximizing inclusive fitness for females is relatively straightforward—find a mate to provide for and protect the offspring until they can reproduce and send the genes of the mother on to the next generation.

Would that the situation were so unambiguous for males, but such is not the case. While pairbonding increases a woman's inclusive fitness, it may not do so for a man, who after all, could spread his genes far more widely by mating with as many women as possible. That most men historically have not done so stems from biological and social reasons. As to the former, the evolution in the human female of continuous sexual receptivity helps hold a man to a woman. So, too, does concealed ovulation—the absence of estrus—that means a man cannot be sure which of his sexual acts results in conception. To ensure that his genes survive, he must seek regular sex with his mate. But biology is not enough: The impulse to go from "dad" to "cad" is always a threat, a threat checked by what evolutionary theorists call "paternity confidence." A man is far more apt to remain with a woman and her children if he has a high degree of confidence that the children, and half their genes, are his. Then, and only then, will investment in these offspring pay off biologically. Hence, historically most cultures have severely punished female adultery because it undermines paternity confidence; simultaneously, most cultures extol the importance of marriage and fatherly investment in children. Marriage ensures the husband exclusive sexual access to his wife, which promotes a high degree of paternal confidence and reduces violence among men competing for the same woman.[6]

Nothing in the American past belies the persuasiveness of bioevolutionary theory. In fact, interpreting the sexual history of the United States through the lens of bioevolutionary theory suggests the many steps taken to shore up "paternity confidence" and men's commitment to wives and children in general. Authorities harshly punished adulterous females and condemned predatory male sexuality; marriage received powerful cultural endorsement; law and custom discouraged divorce; and parenthood functioned as a cultural marker of maturity and independence. A number of works on the history of the American family and sexuality bear out the truth of these observations. Legal sanctions against female adultery, for example, were always more draconian than those against males. The double standard, in fact, has a long history in American life as evidenced in legal codes, prescriptive literature, and the actual behavior of men and women.[7] In regulating female sexual behavior more stringently than male, law and its accompanying ideology helped shore up men's paternal confidence.

Although female sexual impropriety received more attention than that of male, the latter, too, felt the sting of official control. While cuckolding other men may make sense biologically, such behavior invites retaliation and may precipitate a dangerous response. Thus, law and culture condemned men who had sex with other men's wives and offered a variety of legal remedies when such lamentable acts occurred.[8] Nor did predatory sexuality in general escape social regulation. Colonial society sought a variety of ways to contain male sexuality, and by the early nineteenth century moral reform movements explicitly sought to hold men to a female-inspired, single standard of sexual morality. Until well into the twentieth century, sexuality for both men and women could not be disentangled from the marital, reproductive matrix that gave it cultural meaning.[9]

Of course, one need not resort to complicated bioevolutionary perspectives to prove that fathers and children lived together more often in the past than they do today. Even a cursory look at demographic data proves the point; soaring rates of divorce and out-of-wedlock birth since the mid-1960s have reshaped family life in ways that often separate men from their offspring. My point in bringing a bioevolutionary perspective into view is simply to show how fundamental this demographic change is, how it runs counter not only to America's prior history but to the evolution of the species itself. And while we may find exceptions to this coresidence of fathers and children—high mortality rates in the early Chesapeake Bay area, for example, made such bonds fragile—these exceptions prove the rule. Until recently, American culture for both historical and bioevolutionary reasons powerfully endorsed the father-child bond, and what we have today is a unique challenge to this endorsement.

PATERNAL AVAILABILITY

The second major assumption about fatherhood in the past is that fathers spent time with their children and played an important role in shaping their offsprings' development. At one level, this assumption seems easy to confirm; surely farmers, artisans, and small-town day laborers saw their children more often than harried, overworked factory workers and corporate bureaucrats. Yet the reality and meaning of paternal availability in the past is not altogether clear. Until we have more research, just how much time fathers and children actually spent together remains a matter of conjecture. Certainly, paternal availability varied enormously by race and class. Farmers no doubt spent considerable time with their children, but even here we read of men who spent long periods away from home, of plantation owners who, in pursuit of business or political interests, seldom saw their children. Farther down the social scale, fathers periodically left the home in search of work. Hispanic men in New Mexico, as Sarah Deutsch has shown, left their wives and children for long periods of time, a peripatetic fate shared by other Black and White workingmen.[10] In Boston women headed a surprisingly high percentage of families in White working-class neighborhoods, and among Blacks, females headed 25 percent or more of all households.[11] The instability of life for most working-class families throughout American history, coupled with the well-known hardships of millions of rural families, caution against overestimating the intergenerational bonding of fathers and children. Periodic un- and underemployment, financial panics, technological change, overproduction, wide-spread farm problems, and a host of other factors undermined men's availability to their children.

The culture of the "self-made man" did the same. Michael Kimmel and Anthony Rotundo have described in detail the emergence of a nineteenth-century conception of manhood predicated on relentless striving for personal autonomy. A man measured his worth by his ability to succeed in a highly competitive business world, an effort predicated on diligence, sobriety, self-control, and steadiness of character. Self-made men constantly had to prove their manhood to their peers, especially their working peers. The workplace was a masculine realm, the home a feminine one, and workingmen and businessmen alike increasingly spent time away from their wives and children. In a society dominated by market values and the pursuit of material well-being, how else to prove one's manliness but to devote oneself to work?[12] How else to gain the status of "breadwinner" and the implied maturity and social standing that came with it unless one spent long hours away from home?

To achieve such standing, fathers and children often parted ways. Anxieties about paternal availability, in fact, go back at least to the rise of a commercial, industrial economy that generated a series of social and ideological changes that valorized motherhood and marginalized fatherhood. From the early nineteenth century on, motherhood was ascendant, fatherhood in eclipse, and this dynamic prompted repeated efforts to connect, or reconnect, men to their children. Thus, we find moralists as early as the 1830s and 1840s calling men back to the home and lamenting their long hours in factories and offices, their excessive involvement in politics, their proclivity to spend leisure time with other men. Behind such exhortations is a lament, a sense that men were drifting away from the home, a point made in 1842 by the Reverend John Abbott, a Calvinist pastor from Worcester, Massachusetts, in words that seem strikingly modern: "[P]aternal neglect is at the present time one of the most abundant sources of domestic sorrow."[13] Throughout the nineteenth and twentieth centuries, a host of family authorities shared Abbott's anxieties. Medical writers in the 1870s and 1880s suggested that fatherhood helped to curb men's self-indulgence and immaturity and disciplined their sexual desire. Begetting children made men less selfish and more refined and virile.[14] Fatherhood was literally good for men's health. Advice in popular literature made much the same case and urged men to spend "quality" time with their offspring. As I have shown elsewhere, these sentiments developed by the 1920s into the "new fatherhood," an ideology born from a host of economic, class, and social changes and from widely shared cultural anxieties about men's place within the family.[15] Not the least among the latter was the belief that men must find a new basis of connection to their children, one based on companionship and mutuality. Lurking behind such advice were well-placed fears that men ignored their children and forfeited child guidance to mothers, sentiments that made sense given work pressures and the tendency of men to spend their free hours with other men.[16]

I am not attempting to "define deviancy downward" here. I am arguing neither that today's problem of fatherlessness is illusory nor that it is simply an old problem in a new guise. I am not denying that the demographic revolution is real. Millions of men walk out on their children, never know the children they beget, or, for whatever reason, lack contact with their children. Having said this, my point is simply to raise cautionary flags, to suggest that today's debate about fatherlessness often is cast against a mythic past, a past in which all families were headed by resident fathers who spent great amounts of time with their children. Clearly, such was not the case for slave fathers, immigrant men on the move, impoverished farmers looking for factory work, men who worked sixty to seventy hours per week away from home, or fathers who simply faded into the urban landscape and left their wives and children to fend for themselves. It was not even true for well-heeled middle-class men who struggled to prove their masculinity in the workplace and then spent evenings in the company of their "brothers" at the fraternal lodge.[17]

FATHERHOOD AND PATRIARCHY

The third major assumption about fatherhood in the past—that cultural coherence prevailed, that men knew what was expected of them and did their duty, that men were "good enough"—is even more problematic. This vision of the past must be examined in two ways—politically and historically. The first task involves carefully unpacking the relationship among "traditional" family structures, liberal theory, and male domination. Before we uncritically extol the virtues of families in the past, we must uncover the politics on which they rest. The second task requires a brief historical examination of the ideology of fatherhood in order to assess just how seamless an ideal it actually was. I would argue that a strong case can be made that fatherhood as an idea or cultural norm has lacked consistency since at least the early to mid-nineteenth century and that today's confusion merely signifies the long unraveling of fatherhood as a coherent social ideal.

As to the politics of "good-enough" fatherhood, this cultural ideal was and remains predicated on the importance of men's economic independence and women's economic dependence. Throughout the nation's history, most Americans have heartily endorsed the "intact two-parent family" as the normative family structure, one that entails a breadwinning father and a stay-at-home mother. Such families, proponents argue, promote the welfare of children and ultimately the welfare of the state. Children reared in two-parent families are richer, happier, smarter, more popular, and less prone to abuse, neglect, violence, and promiscuity than those reared in single-parent households.[18] They are more likely to be "prepared—intellectually, physically, morally, and emotionally—to take their place as law-abiding and independent citizens."[19]

Why not, then, do everything possible to promote such families? Since independence is a key virtue of a free society, one might argue that government should do all it can to promote it, and the key way to promote independence is to encourage intact, self-reliant families headed by breadwinning males. This is the conservative argument in a nutshell: "Traditional" family structures lay at the heart of freedom and civil society. Through the sacrifices necessary to maintain intact, *independent* families, fathers and mothers embody and promote the very values that make state assistance unnecessary. But there are good reasons to be cautious. If fatherhood gained coherence from this emphasis on intact, independent families headed by men, it was a coherence gained by masking male domination of women. Behind paeans for intact families, as feminist theorist Iris Marion Young points out, stands another assumption. The intact family's virtue resides in its independence from state assistance, independence based historically on breadwinning males who support their dependent wives, who either do not work outside the home, work at less remunerative jobs, or work part time. In turn, women have primary responsibility for child care. To them falls the major responsibility for enabling children, especially sons, to achieve the desirable end of liberal society—an independent life. These assumptions unwittingly relegate mothers to second-class citizenship. For most women even today, to be economically well off is to be "economically dependent on a man."[20]

The praise of two-parent families, Young avers, comes to this: To prefer intact marriages over female-headed families without first considering gender inequalities in earning power and the household division of labor "amounts to calling for mothers to depend on men to keep them out of poverty, and this entails subordination in many cases."[21] After all, power is distributed unequally in families, and the inequality stems most often from the disproportionately higher wages that men bring to the household. Praising independent, intact families all too often means praising dependent women who may, to be sure, live lives of affluence and happiness in some cases but lives of submission and fear in others. Regardless, the underlying theoretical assumption is clear. Economically independent families headed by men—free of state welfare, demanding in services only what they pay in taxes—represent the historic foundation of liberal society and today's vision of the good society among conservative critics. In the latter's estimation, people dependent upon the state are less worthy, less capable of being virtuous citizens. If women do not have husbands and/or well-paid jobs, they cannot be truly independent of the state, and if they cannot be independent of the state, they are parasites—the not "truly needy"—who too often rear disruptive, even criminally inclined children who threaten civil order. It is a profoundly pessimistic vision of America, betraying deep suspicions of women independent of the support of men.[22]

And yet the pessimism goes even deeper. If many family authorities look with suspicion on female-headed families dependent on state assistance, their vision of men without families is equally bleak. Liberal society needs intact families because without them, men and social order devolve into savagery. Underlying conservative social theory is the belief that men, free from marriage and fatherhood, inevitably will become selfish barbarians. Only marriage and fatherhood can discipline men and turn their innate aggressiveness in positive directions. Male violence, David Blankenhorn argues, "is restrained principally by 'paternal investment' in children, achieved through a 'reproductive alliance' with the mother."[23] Without this alliance and investment, men wage war on women and children: "As marriage weakens, more and more men become isolated and estranged from their children and from the mothers of their children. One result, in turn, is the spread of male violence."[24] To prevent such violence, men need discipline, purpose, and commitment that only breadwinning and fatherhood can provide.

But fatherhood does more than prevent men's worst impulses from surfacing. Fathers also provide their children with economic security and prepare their own sons for mature manhood by helping them break from their mothers and gain secure masculine identities.

Without fathers to help sons navigate through troubled psychological waters, the boys become hypermasculine and filled with rage against women: "if we want to learn the identity of the rapist, the hater of women, the occupant of jail cells," writes Blankenhorn, "we do not look first to boys with traditionally masculine fathers. We look first to boys with no fathers."[25] Nor do fathers leave their daughters' lives untouched. Fathers help daughters establish a secure sexual identity and a sense of autonomy that reduces the likelihood of precocious sexual activity and teenage pregnancy.

The praise of two-parent families led by males, then, not only obscures critical assumptions about male power and female dependence but veils even more fundamental anxieties about male psychology and behavior. For conservatives, families headed by men represent the foundation of liberal democratic society and also the best hedge against social anarchy, not only because mothers cannot rear children alone but because men inevitably become predatory unless constrained by marriage and commitment to offspring. No wonder the debate about fatherless families has become so heated. The stakes could scarcely be higher. Those who praise the "traditional family" criticize state intervention in families, reject the modern shift toward more egalitarian relationships between men and women, and stand opposed to efforts to bring the duties and responsibilities of fatherhood and motherhood closer together.[26] Those who reject the traditional family embrace egalitarianism and the androgynous drift, believe in the efficacy of state support for women and families, and are far less pessimistic about the nature of innate male psychology.

THE UNSTABLE IDEAL

If the political and psychological theories underpinning "good-enough" fatherhood require explication, so too does its history, specifically the argument that fathers in the past knew what was expected of them, that cultural coherence prevailed when it came to fatherhood. Again, there is a superficial truth to this argument. Logic would suggest that before the great post–World War II transformations wrought by mothers' movement into the labor force, changing family structures, and the emergence of feminism, men more or less knew what they were supposed to do. They were breadwinners, providers, and role models of manhood. Men may have muddled through their marriages, but they stayed with their wives and children. But the story is complicated here, as well; first, we lack evidence about how men in the past viewed their responsibilities as fathers. Until scholars do more work in this regard, we can only make bold and largely unsubstantiated guesses. My own research from the early decades of the twentieth century suggests that many men were full of doubt as they tried to balance the demands of work with those of the home and as they tried to steer a course between traditional patriarchal prerogatives and newer guidelines concocted by family experts.[27] Second, I think we can say that the twentieth-century discourse on fatherhood reveals anything but coherence. In fact, aside from the belief that men should be primary providers for their offspring and that they should remain married to the mothers of their children, much has been in flux since at least the turn of the century. In addition and closely related, a combination of factors has been eroding the power of men within their families for many years.

Without repeating in detail arguments I have spelled out elsewhere, suffice to say that men's personal control over their children has waned since at least the early years of the industrial revolution. As factory and office work removed men from the home for long periods of the day, as the cultural saliency of motherhood steadily rose, and as various institutions, a growing youth culture, and consumer capitalism increasingly shaped children's lives, men's personal power over their offspring declined. Patriarchal power resided less in the hands of individual men than in the workings of institutions and organizations such as schools, juvenile courts, reform schools, Boy Scouts, and organized sports.[28] Such power also increasingly resided in the hands of experts, university-trained men and women who rarely exhibited self-doubt, whose standards were largely emotional and psychological. Fathers found themselves on the outside looking in as these experts directed most of their attention to mothers while warning men to spend enough time with theirs sons so that the latter would not end up as "sissies" or, worse, homosexuals.[29]

In response to this decline in fatherly authority, social authorities did what had to be done; they redefined the meaning of being a father, and they did so in recognizably modern ways. In the opening decades of this century, social scientists, psychologists, and family experts shared many of the same anxieties evinced in today's debate about fatherlessness. Central to their theory was the belief that family bonds had been weakened by industrialization and urbanization, that fatherly functions and authority had diminished, and that the key task for men now was to help foster the healthy personality development of their children by building families characterized by tolerance, strong emotional bonds, diffuse authority, and companionship. By the 1930s, such ideas had crystallized into a full-blown theory of sex-role socialization predicated on the belief that fatherly involvement with children would help to counteract a dangerous drift toward excessively feminized homes.

World War II and its aftermath required new perspectives on fatherhood as a cultural ideal. With the outbreak of hostilities, experts worried about the impact of the drafting of fathers on social order while psychologists asserted the indispensability of fathers to family life and counseled mothers on how to keep their absent husbands present in the lives of the children. As men began new families or returned to their old ones after the war, experts insisted that fathers imbued with a democratic, permissive, nurturing sensibility could produce well-adjusted offspring capable of resisting the new dangers of the age—authoritarianism, juvenile delinquency, schizophrenia, and homosexuality. In a culture beset by a variety of

Cold War and sexual anxieties, the nurturing father comprised an important line of defense against social disorder. Such nurturing, moreover, became an important marker of social class and a sure sign of "maturity," "responsibility," and manhood itself.

Anxiety, not ideological coherence, characterized the postwar discourse on fatherhood. A combination of breadwinning, liberal politics, and therapeutic impulses gave shape to the postwar variant of the "new fatherhood." While many misread history and suggest that aloof, work-obsessed, conformist drones slogged off to the office before the children were up and returned after they went to bed, the postwar "gray flannel" brigade was, in fact, extraordinarily child-centered, part of a culture that emphasized the importance of fathers to children's personality development, sexual orientation, and, at the most grandiose, the future of democracy.[30] In the midst of anxieties about communism, democracy, homosexuality, and juvenile delinquency, fatherhood became an important locus of cultural concern about the future of the family.

Again, the point is not to suggest that nothing has changed, that fatherhood has always been an unstable cultural concept. To a certain extent, that is true, but the fact remains that changes since the early 1960s have altered the reality and discourse of fatherhood even more significantly. Put differently, the level of instability has not been constant. Since the early 1960s, out-of-wedlock birth rates and divorce rates have soared; men do not spend as much time with children as they used to; and women's movement into the labor force has reconfigured domestic responsibilities for husbands and wives.[31] Social scientists argue over men's contribution to children's development while some on the left wonder about the importance of men at all. For their part, feminists praise the evolution of new family forms while simultaneously urging men to increase their day-to-day care of children.

This welter of ideas about fatherhood signifies how demographic and political change have accelerated the decomposition of fatherhood as a coherent ideal. But it was a decomposition long in the making. Fatherhood and, one might add, masculinity itself have been historically unstable concepts; the profound changes in American family life since World War II did not create but have powerfully added to this instability. Thus, we must not posit a coherence that never existed nor ignore the politics of the male-headed, two-parent family. The first distorts the past and the second turns a blind eye to the oppression of women. We may welcome the return of men to the family, but we must be clear on the terms of their return.

That said, I believe we can find common ground as we think through the problem of fatherlessness. As a start, we need more studies of the history of fatherhood so that we can move beyond mythic and fictive interpretations of how fathers and fatherhood used to be. Nor should the politics of the family ever drift from focus; families headed by breadwinning fathers may be a solution for some, but for others they embody a form of patriarchal power that relegates women to second-class status. Informed by history and attuned to politics, we can begin to make sense of fatherlessness and recognize it as an extraordinarily complicated issue. It will not do to define it away, to pretend that the problem is merely in the minds of Promise Keepers and their cohorts. Too much research suggests that fathers play a vital role in children's psychological, social, intellectual, and moral development. Most fathers, I would argue, know this intuitively and are immediately suspicious of any argument or theory suggesting they do not. Fathers matter; they have in the past, they do now, they will in the future. Saying this does not mean that women cannot rear wonderful children without men, but it does mean that children's lives are deeply enriched by their fathers' presence.

Acknowledging this enrichment, however, does not mean that the solution is to limit divorce, revivify traditional gender relations, and lambast and ridicule the efforts of contemporary fathers to forge more nurturing relations with their children.[32] The factors that have reshaped fatherhood, that have led to fatherlessness, have deep cultural, social, and economic roots. As I have tried to suggest, we must be careful not to overstate the cultural coherence of fatherhood in the past or men's availability to their children. Nor is it likely that divorce or out-of-wedlock birth rates are likely to fall dramatically. These, too, have their sources in critical changes within American society. Nor will liberal feminism, women's workforce participation, or the sexualization of American culture disappear anytime soon. These changes are rooted within the history of American society, and no bromides, quick fixes, or revivals of one stripe or another are likely to make much of a dent.

Given the depth and complexity of the problem, finding a solution to "fatherlessness" seems well nigh impossible. For over a century, writers and experts have sought to make sense out of fatherhood in a world that took men away from their children for most of the day. These authorities have adjusted their theories to changing events—the Great Depression, World War II—and to changing anxieties—homosexuality, juvenile delinquency—while holding true to a belief in the importance of breadwinning and a gendered division of labor. But even these certainties have fallen over the last forty years thanks to the massive movement of mothers into the labor force and to the revival of feminism with its sustained critique of patriarchy within the workplace and the family.

Meanwhile, fathers have struggled to remain central to the lives of their children despite a series of developments over the course of the twentieth century that have continually eroded men's authority and presence within their families. The emergence of an advanced consumer society, the growing predominance of a therapeutic culture, the relocation of parental authority within institutions, the rise of the youth culture; even the availability of radios, televisions, movies, and automobiles have all played a part in disconnecting men from their children long before the current demographic revolution took place that has literally moved men away from their offspring. Confronted by these changes, both family experts and actual fathers struggle to find a mode of fatherhood that makes sense. For some, it has been the adoption of the tenets of feminism; for others, conservative Christianity; for most, an effort to combine the traditional prerogatives of breadwinning with the new demands of a changing household economy.

Whatever the perspective, we need not throw up our hands in despair. Surely we can reject the idea that fathers are superfluous without simultaneously reinvigorating old-time fatherhood and skewering those trying to build more egalitarian forms of parenting. At the same time, we should approach with caution the therapeutic impulses of the "new fatherhood" and avoid hiding hard choices behind a screen of good cheer and optimistic blather. Above all, we must continue to reflect on a problem central to liberal theory and modern individualism: how to balance the self-interest of adults with the needs of children. Any number of small steps can be taken. As a society, we can try to teach young men and women to be sexually responsible; we might as well try to help young parents withstand the financial pressures that so often break up marriages; and we can encourage men to spend more time with their children and to do more day-to-day child care. We can try to discourage divorce or make it tougher to obtain for those with children, and we certainly can establish divorce procedures and policies that try to keep fathers a presence in the lives of their children. We can try any number of things, but we must be aware that such remedies confront a problem that will not be solved easily. The past can offer insight into the origins of fatherlessness, but it cannot offer a solution that comes with acceptable costs. Unless we are ready to endorse a politics of the family that relegates women to a subordinate position, our solutions to the problem of fatherlessness must be based on building gender relations predicated on equality.

NOTES

1. During the last decade, newspapers and magazines have been full of information on the new fatherhood; moreover, workshops and seminars abound and a host of organizations, including Promise Keepers, seek to create closer bonds between fathers and their children. A now-dated directory that reveals the number and scope of such organizations is Debra G. Klinman and Rhiana Kohl, *Fatherhood U.S.A.* (New York: Garland, 1984).

2. David Blankenhorn, *Fatherless America: Confronting Our Most Urgent Social Problem* (New York: Basic Books, 1995); David Popenoe, *Life without Father: Compelling New Evidence that Fatherhood and Marriage Are Indispensable for the Good of Children and Society* (New York: Free Press, 1996).

3. Blankenhorn, *Fatherless America,* 18-22, 202-11.

4. Popenoe, *Life without Father,* 166. My analysis of the bioevolutionary perspective is drawn from Popenoe's lucid summary.

5. Jane Lancaster and Chet Lancaster, "The Watershed: Change in Parental-Investment and Family Formation Strategies in the Course of Human Evolution," in Lancaster et al., eds. *Parenting Across the Life Span: Biosocial Dimensions* (New York: Aldine DeGruyter, 1987), 192, quoted in Popenoe, *Life without Father,* 170.

6. While cuckolding men and getting them to rear your genetic offspring may make sense biologically, such behavior invites them to do the same and may precipitate a dangerous response. Thus, the "dad" strategy, with its paternal confidence, investment, and potential for male cooperation rather than violence, seems the more reasonable strategy. On this point, see Popenoe, *Life without Father,* 176-77.

7. For an excellent overview of the history of sexuality in America, see John D'Emilio and Estelle B. Freedman, *Intimate Matters: A History of Sexuality in America* (New York: Harper & Row, 1988).

8. Sanctions could range from alienation-of-affection suits, to divorce, to justifiable homicide. On law and the family, see Michael Grossberg, *Governing the Hearth: Law and the Family in Nineteenth-Century America* (Chapel Hill: University of North Carolina Press, 1985), and Robert L. Griswold, "Law, Sex, Cruelty, and Divorce in Victorian America, 1840-1900," *American Quarterly* 38 (Winter 1986): 721-45. On justifiable homicide, see Angus McLaren, *The Trials of Masculinity: Policing Sexual Boundaries* (Chicago: University of Chicago Press, 1997), 111-132.

9. 9. D'Emilio and Freedman, *Intimate Matters,* 222-76.

10. Sarah Deutsch, *No Separate Refuge: Culture, Class, and Gender on an Anglo-Hispanic Frontier in the American Southwest, 1880-1940* (New York: Oxford University Press, 1987), 41-62.

11. On White household structure, see Linda Gordon, *Heroes of Their Own Lives: The Politics and History of Family Violence* (New York: Penguin, 1988),

92-95. Elizabeth Pleck offers a useful summary of the data on Black household structure in *Black Migration and Poverty: Boston, 1865-1900* (New York: Academic Press, 1979), 183-84.

12. Michael Kimmel, *Manhood in America: A Cultural History* (New York: Free Press, 1996), 13-80; Anthony Rotundo, *American Manhood: Transformation in Masculinity from the Revolution to the Present Era* (New York: Basic Books, 1993), 18-25; on consumption and the rise of the middle class, see Stuart Blumin, *The Emergence of the Middle Class: Social Experience in the Industrializing City, 1760-1900* (Cambridge: Cambridge University Press, 1989), 138-191, 275-290; and on consumption and fatherhood, see Griswold, *Fatherhood in America*, 134-141. David Leverenz analyzes the relationship among individualism, work, and male competitiveness in *Manhood and the American Renaissance* (Ithaca, NY: Cornell University Press, 1989), 72-90.

13. John Abbott, "Paternal Nelgect," *The Parents' Magazine and Young Peoples' Friend* (Concord, NH, 1842) quoted in Stephen Frank, "Life with Father: Parenthood and Masculinity in the Nineteenth-Century American North," Ph.D. Diss., University of Michigan, 1995, 49.

14. Frank, "Life with Father," 77-88.

15. On the "new fatherhood" of the early twentieth century, see Griswold, *Fatherhood in America*, 88-142.

16. On men and leisure, see Mark Carnes, *Secret Ritual and Manhood in Victorian America* (New Haven, CT: Yale University Press, 1989), Ted Ownby, *Subduing Satan: Religion, Recreation and Manhood in the Rural South* (Chapel Hill: University of North Carolina Press, 1991), 21-99; Roy Rosenzweig, *Eight Hours for What We Will: Workers and Leisure in an Industrial City, 1870-1920* (Cambridge: Cambridge University Press, 1983), 35-64; and Jon M. Kingsdale, "The `Poor Man's Club': Social Functions of the Urban Working-Class Saloon," *American Quarterly* 25 (October 1975): 472-489.

17. Carnes' book *Secret Ritual* explores Victorian men's involvement in fraternal organizations in a highly imaginative and provocative way. It is clear from his analysis that these organizations took many men away from home for several nights each week.

18. Both Blankenhorn and Popenoe summarize the massive social science literature on fathers and families and conclude that fathers play a vital role in the development of their children's well-being. For an exhaustive, although now somewhat dated, overview of this literature, see Michael Lamb, "Fathers and Child Development: An Integrative Overview," in Lamb, ed., *The Role of the Father in Child Development* (New York: Wiley, 1981), 1-70.

19. This quotation by William Galston from his book *Liberal Purposes* (Cambridge: Cambridge University Press, 1991) is quoted in Iris Marion Young, "Mothers, Citizenship, and Independence: A Critique of Pure Family Values," *Ethics* 105 (April 1995): 537.

20. Young, "Mothers, Citizenship, and Independence," 544.

21. Ibid., 545.

22. Blankenhorn, *Fatherless America,* 26-48; also, Popenoe, *Life without Father,* 52-80. Popenoe titles this chapter "The Human Carnage of Fatherlessness."

23. Blankenhorn, *Fatherless America,* 34. Blankenhorn is here drawing on a cross-cultural study of homicide by Martin Daly and Margo Wilson.

24. Ibid., 38.

25. Ibid., 31.

26. Many scholars have noted conservatives' suspicion of men's basic nature and the need for marriage and children as a "civilizing" influence. One of the most interesting is Barbara Ehrenreich, *The Hearts of Men: American Dreams and the Flight from Commitment* (New York: Anchor, 1983), 161-168. For examples of such suspicions, see Blankenhorn, *Fatherless America,* 26-42, Popenoe, *Life without Father,* 61-63, 73-76, George Gilder, *Sexual Suicide* (New York: Quadrangle, 1973), 97, and George Gilder, *Wealth and Poverty* (New York: Basic Books, 1981), 69-70.

27. Griswold, *Fatherhood in America,* 119-142.

28. Ibid., 56-66, 81-87; Kimmel, *Manhood in America,* 117-156.

29. Griswold, *Fatherhood in America,* 120-132.

30. The foregoing analysis has drawn heavily on chapters 5-6 and 8-9 of Ibid.

31. Ibid., 219-242. Two scholars have calculated the actual reduction in time men spend in the company of small children; see David Eggebeen and Peter Uhlenberg, "Changes in the Organization of Men's Lives: 1960-1980,: *Family Relations* 34 (April 1985): 251-57.

32. Blankenhorn's criticism of the "new fatherhood" is in *Fatherless America,* 96-123.

Two

LIFE WITHOUT FATHER

David Popenoe

THE DECLINE OF FATHERHOOD is one of the most basic, unexpected, and extraordinary trends of our time. Its dimensions can be captured in a single statistic: In just three decades, between 1960 and 1990, the percentage of children living apart from their natural fathers more than doubled, from 17 percent to 36 percent. If this trend continues, by early in the next century nearly half of all American children will be going to sleep each evening without being able to say good night to their dads.

No one predicted this trend; few researchers or government agencies have monitored it; and it is not widely discussed, even today. But the decline of fatherhood is a major force behind many of the most disturbing problems that plague American society: crime and juvenile delinquency; premature sexuality and out-of-wedlock births to teenagers; deteriorating educational achievement; depression, substance abuse, and alienation among adolescents; and the growing number of women and children in poverty.

The current generation of children and youth may be the first in our nation's history to be less well-off—psychologically, socially, economically, and morally—than their parents were at the same age. Indeed, as Senator Daniel Patrick Moynihan has observed, "the United States may be the first society in history in which children are distinctly worse off than adults."[1]

Even as this calamity unfolds, our cultural view of fatherhood itself is changing. Few people doubt the fundamental importance of mothers. But fathers? More and more, the question of whether fathers are really necessary is being raised. Many would answer no, or maybe not. And to the degree that fathers are still thought necessary, fatherhood is said by many to be merely a social role that others can play: mothers, partners, stepfathers, uncles and aunts, grandparents. Perhaps the script can even be rewritten and the role changed—or dropped.

There was a time in the past when fatherlessness was far more common than it is today, but death was to blame, not divorce and out-of-wedlock births. In early seventeenth-century Virginia, only an estimated 31 percent of White children reached age eighteen with both parents still alive.[2] Today, well over 90 percent of America's youngsters reach eighteen with two living parents. Almost all of today's fatherless children have fathers who are alive, well, and perfectly capable of shouldering the responsibilities of fatherhood. Who would ever have thought that so many men would choose to relinquish them?

Not so long ago, the change in the cause of fatherlessness was dismissed as irrelevant in many quarters, including among social scientists. Children, it was said, were merely losing their parents in a different way than they used to. You don't hear that very much anymore. A surprising finding of recent social science research is that it is decidedly worse for a child to lose a father in the modern, voluntary way than through death. The children of divorce and never-married mothers are less successful in life by almost every measure than the children of widowed mothers.[3] The replacement of death by divorce as the prime cause of fatherlessness, then, is a monumental setback in the history of childhood.

Until the 1960s, the falling death rate and the rising divorce rate neutralized each other. In 1900, the percentage of all American children living in single-parent families was 8.5 percent. By 1960, it had increased to just 9.1 percent. But then the decline in the death rate slowed, and the divorce rate skyrocketed. "The scale of marital breakdowns in the West since 1960 has no historical precedent that I know of, and seems unique," says Lawrence Stone, the noted Princeton University family historian. "There has been nothing like it for the last 2,000 years, and probably longer."[4]

In theory, divorce need not mean disconnection. In reality, it often does. One large survey in the late 1980s found that about one in five divorced fathers had not seen his children the past year, and less than half of divorced fathers saw their children more than several times a year.[5] A 1981 survey of adolescents who were living apart from their fathers found that 52 percent had not seen them at all in more than a year; only 16 percent saw their fathers as often as once a week.[6]

The picture grows worse. Just as divorce has overtaken death as the leading cause of fatherlessness, out-of-wedlock births are expected to surpass divorce later in the 1990s. They accounted for 32 percent of all births by 1995, an increase from a mere 5 percent in 1960. And there is substantial evidence that having an unmarried father is even worse for a child than having a divorced father.

FATHERS: ESSENTIAL BUT PROBLEMATIC

Across time and cultures, fathers have always been considered essential—and not just for their sperm. Marriage and the nuclear family—mother, father, and children—are the most universal social institutions in existence. In no society has the birth of children out of wedlock been the cultural norm. To the contrary, a concern for the legitimacy of children is nearly universal.

At the same time, being a father is universally problematic for men. While mothers the world over bear and nurture their young with an intrinsic acknowledgment and, most commonly, acceptance of their role, the process of taking on the role of father is often filled with conflict and doubt. The source of this sex-role difference can be plainly stated. Men are not biologically as attuned to being committed fathers as women are to being committed mothers. The evolutionary logic is clear. Women, who can bear only a limited number of children, have a great incentive to invest their energy in rearing children, while men, who can father many offspring, do not. Left culturally unregulated, men's sexual behavior can be promiscuous, their paternity casual, their commitment to families weak.[7]

This is not to say that the role of father is foreign to male nature. Far from it. Evolutionary scientists tell us that the development of the fathering capacity and high paternal investments in offspring—features not common among our primate relatives—have been sources of enormous evolutionary advantage for human beings.

In recognition of the fatherhood problem, human cultures have used sanctions to bind men to their children, and of course the institution of marriage has been culture's chief vehicle. Marriage is society's way of signaling that the community approves and encourages sexual intercourse and the birth of children, and that the long-term relationship of the parents is socially important.

FATHERLESSNESS AND CHILDREN

In my many years as a sociologist, I have found few other bodies of evidence that lean so much in one direction as this one: On the whole, two parents—a father and a mother—are better for a child than one parent. There are, to be sure, many factors that complicate this simple proposition. We all know of a two-parent family that is truly dysfunctional—the proverbial family from hell. A child can certainly be raised to a fulfilling adulthood by one loving parent who is devoted to the child's well-being. But such exceptions do not invalidate the rule any more than the fact that some three-pack-a-day smokers live to a ripe old age casts doubt on the dangers of cigarettes.

The collapse of children's well-being in the United States has reached breathtaking proportions. Juvenile violent crime has increased sixfold, from 16,000 arrests in 1960 to 96,000 in 1992. Eating disorders and rates of depression have soared among adolescent girls. Teen suicide has tripled. Alcohol and drug abuse among teenagers, although it has leveled off in recent years, continues at a very high rate. Poverty has shifted from the elderly to the young. Of all the nation's poor today, 38 percent are children.[8]

One can think of many explanations for these unhappy developments: the growth of commercialism and consumerism, the influence of television and the mass media, the decline of religion, the widespread availability of guns and addictive drugs, and the decay of social order and neighborhood relationships. None of these causes should be dismissed. But the evidence is now strong that the absence of fathers from the lives of children is one of the most important causes.

The most tangible and immediate consequence of fatherlessness for children is the loss of economic resources. By the best recent estimates, the income of the household in which a child remains after a divorce instantly declines by about 21 percent per capita on average, while expenses tend to go up.[9] Over time, the economic situation for the child often deteriorates further.

The proliferation of mother-headed families now constitutes something of a national economic emergency. About one-quarter of all family groups with children—more than half of all Black family groups—are headed by mothers, which is more than double the 11.5 percent figure in 1970.[10] No other group is so poor, and none stays poor longer. Poverty afflicts nearly one out of every two of these families, but fewer than one in ten married-couple families. In recent years, mother-headed families have accounted for 94 percent of caseloads for Aid to Families with Dependent Children (AFDC).[11]

Economic difficulties—which translate into poorer schooling and other handicaps—ultimately account for a considerable share of the disadvantages found among fatherless children. By the best recent estimates, however, economic status accounts for no more than half of these disadvantages. The latest and most authoritative review of the research concluded that children who grow up with only one of their biological parents (nearly always the mother) are twice as likely to drop out of high school, 2.5 times as likely to become teen mothers, and 1.4 times as likely to be idle—out of school and out of work—as children who grow up with both parents.[12]

Such conclusions will no longer come as a surprise to many Americans. Yet it was not so long ago that the divorce revolution was given a strangely positive cast in American popular culture. If breaking up is better for parents, it was thought, it cannot be all that bad for children. What keeps parents happy should also keep children happy.[13] In part, this was a convenient, guilt-retarding rationalization for parents who were breaking up. Recent evidence throws such sentiments in serious doubt.

WHAT DO FATHERS DO?

Few people doubt the fundamental importance of mothers, but what do fathers do? Much of what they contribute to the growth of their children, of course, is simply the result of being a second adult in the home. Bringing up children is demanding, stressful, and often exhausting. Two adults cannot only support and spell each other; they can offset each other's deficiencies and build on each other's strengths.

Fathers also bring an array of unique qualities to parenting roles. Some of these roles are familiar: protector and role model. Teenage boys without fathers are notoriously prone to trouble. The pathway to adulthood for daughters is somewhat easier, but they still must learn from their fathers, in ways they cannot from their mothers, how to relate to men. They learn from their fathers about heterosexual trust, intimacy, and difference. They learn to appreciate their own femininity from the one male who is most special in their lives. Most important, through loving and being loved by their fathers, they learn that they are love-worthy.

Recent research has given us much deeper—and more surprising—insights into the father's role in child rearing.[14] It shows that in almost all of their interactions with children, fathers do things a little differently from mothers. What fathers do—their special parenting style—is not only highly complementary to what mothers do but is by all indications important in its own right for optimum child rearing.

For example, an often-overlooked dimension of fathering is play. From their children's birth through adolescence, the father's style of play seems to have unusual significance. It is likely to be both physically stimulating and exciting. With older children it involves more physical games and teamwork requiring the competitive testing of physical and mental skills. It frequently resembles an apprenticeship or teaching relationship: Come on, let me show you how.

Mothers typically spend more time playing with their children, but theirs is a different kind of play. Mothers' play tends to take place more at the child's level. Mothers provide the child with the opportunity to direct the play, to be in charge, to proceed at the child's own pace.

The way fathers play has effects on everything from the management of emotions to intelligence and academic achievement. It is particularly important in promoting self-control. According to one expert, "children who roughhouse with their fathers quickly learn that biting, kicking and other forms of physical violence are not acceptable."[15] They learn when to "shut it down."

A committee assembled by the Board on Children and Families of the National Research Council concluded children "learn critical lessons about how to recognize and deal with highly charged emotions in the context of playing with their fathers. Fathers, in effect, give children practice in regulating their own emotions and recognizing others' emotional clues."[16] The findings of a study of convicted murderers in Texas are probably not the product of coincidence: 90 percent of them either did not play as children or played abnormally.[17]

At play and in other realms, fathers tend to stress competition, challenge, initiative, risk-taking, and independence. Mothers, in contrast, stress emotional security and personal safety. On the playground, fathers will try to get the child to swing ever higher, higher than the person on the next swing, while mothers will be cautious, worrying about accidents.

It is sometimes said that fathers express more concern for the child's longer-term development, while mothers focus on the child's immediate well-being (which, of course, in its own way has everything to do with a child's long-term well-being). What is clear is that children have dual needs that must be met. Becoming a mature and competent adult involves the integration of two often-contradictory human desires: for communion, or the feeling of being included, connected, and related, and for agency, which entails individuality and independence. One without the other is a denuded and impaired humanity, an incomplete realization of the human potential.[18]

For some couples, to be sure, these functions are not rigidly divided along standard female-male lines. There may even be a role reversal in some cases, with men largely assuming the female style and women the male style. But these are exceptions that prove the rule. Gender-differentiated parenting is of such importance that in child rearing by homosexual couples, either gay or lesbian, one partner commonly fills the male-instrumental role while the other fills the female-expressive role.

It is ironic, however, that in our public discussion of fathering, it is seldom acknowledged that fathers have a distinctive role to play. Indeed, far more often it is said that fathers should be more like mothers. While this is said with the best of intentions, the effects are perverse. After all, if fathering is no different from mothering, males can easily be replaced in the home by women. It might even seem better to do so. Already viewed as a burden and obstacle to self-fulfillment, fatherhood thus comes to seem superfluous and unnecessary as well.

FATHERLESSNESS AND SOCIAL PROBLEMS

What fathers do, and do not do, is directly implicated in many of our most grievous social ills. Of all the negative consequences of father absence, juvenile delinquency and violence—too many little boys with guns—probably loom largest in the public mind. Reported violent crime has soared 550 percent since 1960, and juveniles have had the fastest-growing crime rate. For example, arrests of juveniles for murder rose 128 percent between 1983 and 1992.

Many people intuitively believe that fatherlessness is related to delinquency and violence, and the weight of research evidence supports this belief.[19] Having a father at home is no guarantee that a youngster will not commit a crime, but it appears to be an excellent form of protection. In America, 60 percent of rapists, 72 percent of adolescent murderers, and 70 percent of long-term prison inmates come from fatherless homes.[20]

Fathers are important to their sons as role models. They are important for maintaining authority and discipline. And they are important in helping their sons to develop both self-control and feelings of empathy toward others, character traits that are found to be lacking in violent youth.

The twin to the nightmare specter of too many little boys with guns is too many little girls with babies. During the past three decades, there has been a dramatic increase in the percentage of teenagers engaging in sexual activity. About one million teen pregnancies occur in the United States each year, giving this nation the highest teen pregnancy rate in the industrialized world.

Fatherlessness is again a major contributing factor. For example, analyzing data from the National Child Development Study, a major British longitudinal study that followed the lives of thousands of children born in 1958, researcher Kathleen Kiernan found that young women with divorced or separated parents are more likely to form unions in their teens, to have a child at an early age, and to bear children outside of marriage. Kiernan highlighted one important characteristic that opens the door to other problems: Girls from single-parent families are more likely to leave home at an early age than other girls.[21]

Fathers are the first and most important men in the lives of girls. They provide male role models, accustoming their daughters to male-female relationships. Engaged and responsive fathers play with their daughters and guide them into challenging activities. They protect them, providing them with a sense of physical and emotional security. Girls with adequate fathering are more able, as they grow older, to develop constructive heterosexual relationships based on trust and intimacy.

On the face of it, there would seem to be at least one potentially positive side to fatherlessness: Without a father around the house, the incidence of child abuse might be expected to drop. Unfortunately, reports of child neglect and abuse have skyrocketed since 1976. One of the greatest risk factors in child abuse, found by virtually every investigation that has ever been conducted, is family disruption, especially living in a female-headed single-parent household.[22] Most of the perpetrators of sexual abuse are men. But less than half of the offenders are family members and close relatives. Ten to 30 percent are strangers, and the remainder are acquaintances of various kinds, including neighbors, peers, and mother's boyfriends.

Why does living without a father pose such hazards for children? Two explanations are usually given: The children receive less supervision and protection from men their mothers bring home, and they are also more emotionally deprived, which leaves them vulnerable to sexual abusers who entrap them by offering affection, attention, and friendship. Even a diligent absent father can't supervise or protect his children the way a live-in father can. Nor is he likely to have the kind of relationship with his daughter that is usually needed to give her a foundation of emotional security and a model for nonsexual relationships with men.[23]

FATHERHOOD, MARRIAGE, AND MEN

The benefits of active fatherhood do not all flow to the child. Men, too, suffer grievously from the growth of fatherlessness. The world over, young and unattached young males have always been a cause for social concern. They can be a danger to themselves and to society. Young unattached men tend to be more aggressive, violent, promiscuous, and prone to substance abuse; they are also more likely to die prematurely through disease, accidents, or self-neglect. They make up the majority of deviants, delinquents, criminals, killers, drug users, vice lords, and miscreants of every kind. Wherever large numbers of young unattached males are concentrated in one place, the probability of social disorder greatly increases. Two trenchant examples are the nineteenth-century American frontier West and the late twentieth-century inner-city ghetto.[24]

Family life—marriage and child rearing—is an extremely important civilizing force for men. It encourages them to develop those habits of character—including prudence, cooperativeness, honesty, trust, and self-sacrifice—that can lead to achievement as an economic provider. Marriage also focuses male sexual energy. Having children typically impresses on men the importance of setting a good example. Who hasn't heard at least one man say that he gave up irresponsible actions only when he married and had children?

Empirical evidence exists to substantiate these reports. One longitudinal study of the first two years of fatherhood found that prior to fatherhood, the men's identities centered on independence, aggressiveness, and self-concerns, whereas following fatherhood, their identities included strong elements of caring and empathy.[25] Another longitudinal study of men found that fatherhood promoted male maturity, especially the ability of men to integrate their own feelings and to understand others sympathetically.[26]

The civilizing effect of being a father is highlighted by a pathbreaking social improvement endeavor in Cleveland. In the inner-city Cleveland neighborhood of Hough, social worker Charles Ballard has been turning around the lives of young Black men through his Institute for Responsible Fatherhood and Family Revitalization. Since 1982, using an intensive social work approach that includes home visits, parenting programs, and group therapy sessions, he has reunited more than 2,000 absent, unwed fathers with their children.

The standard theory is that if you want inner-city men like these to be responsible fathers, you first must find them a job. But Ballard has stood this theory on its head. His approach is that you first must convince the young men of the importance of being a good father, and then they will be motivated to finish school and find work.

An independent evaluation of his approach showed that it really works. Only 12 percent of the young men had full-time work when they entered his program, but 62 percent later found such work and another 12 percent found part-time jobs. Also, 97 percent of the men he dealt with began providing financial support for their children, and 71 percent had no additional children out of wedlock.[27]

Marriage by itself, even without the presence of children, is also a major civilizing force for men. No other institution save religion (and perhaps the military) places such moral demands on men. To be sure, there is a selection factor in marriage. Those men whom women would care to marry already have some of the civilized virtues. And those men who are morally beyond the pale have difficulty finding mates. Yet epidemiological studies and social surveys have shown that marriage has a civilizing effect independent of the selection factor. Marriage actually promotes health, competence, virtue, and personal well-being.[28] With the continued growth of fatherlessness, we can expect to see a nation of men who are at worst morally out of control and at best unhappy, unhealthy, and unfulfilled.

FATHERHOOD AND WOMEN

Another group that has suffered in the new age of fatherlessness is, of course, women. There is no doubt that many women get along very well without men in their lives and that having the wrong men in their lives can be unfortunate, even disastrous. But just as it seems to increase assaults on children, fatherlessness appears to generate more violence against women.

Partly this is a matter of arithmetic. More than two-thirds of violence (assault, robbery, and rape) against women is committed by unrelated acquaintances or strangers.[29] As the number of unattached males in the population goes up, so does the incidence of violence toward women.

Or consider the fact that, of the violence toward women that is committed by intimates and other relatives, only 29 percent involves a current spouse, whereas 42 percent involves a close friend or partner and another 12 percent an ex-spouse.[30] As husbands are replaced by nonspouses and exes, violence toward women increases.

In fact, marriage appears to be a strong safety factor for women. A satisfactory marriage between sexually faithful partners, especially when they are raising their own children, engenders fewer risks for violence than probably any other circumstance in which a woman could find herself. Recent surveys of violent-crime victimization have found that only 12.6 of every 1,000 married women fall victim to violence, compared with 43.9 of every 1,000 never-married women and 66.5 of every 1,000 divorced or separated women.[31]

REESTABLISHING FATHERHOOD AND MARRIAGE

Just as cultural forms can be discarded, dismantled, and declared obsolete, so can they be regenerated. In order to restore marriage and reinstate fathers in the lives of their children, we are somehow going to have to undo the cultural shift of the past few decades toward radical individualism. We can't return to the so-called Ozzie and Harriet, breadwinner-housewife family of the 1950s; that time has passed. And no one wants to return to loveless marriages held together only by economic interdependence. But there are ways to strengthen the institution of marriage and thereby the husband-wife nuclear family that stays together and actively and responsibly raises its children.

Employers, for example, can provide generous parental leave and experiment with more flexible work hours. Religious leaders can reclaim moral ground from the culture of divorce and nonmarriage by resisting the temptation to equate "committed relationships" with marriage. Family scholars and educators can avoid equating the intact, two-parent family with "alternative lifestyles." Marriage counselors can begin with a bias *in favor of* marriage, stressing the needs of the family at least as much as the needs of the client. Legislators can remove marriage penalties from the tax codes and provide more favorable tax treatment for child-rearing couples. As for the entertainment industry, pressure already is being brought to curtail the glamorization of unwed motherhood, marital infidelity, and sexual promiscuity. This pressure should be dramatically expanded.

Premarital education and marital enrichment programs should be expanded across the land. We should consider a two-tier system of divorce law: Marriages without underage children would be relatively easy to dissolve, but marriages with younger children would be subject to stricter guidelines. Longer waiting periods for divorcing couples with children might be called for, combined with greater access to marriage counseling.

The father's role must also be redefined in a way that neglects neither historical models nor unique attributes of modern societies, the new roles for women, and the special qualities that men bring to child rearing. Above all, fathers should be taught that fathering is more than merely providing food, clothing, and shelter to children and letting mothers take care of the rest. Fathers should become fully engaged in their children's social and psychological development from day one and provide their children with continuing reassurance of their love and devotion.

What the decline of fatherhood and marriage in America really means is that slowly, insidiously, and relentlessly our society has been moving in an ominous direction. If we are to make progress toward a more just and humane society, we must reverse the tide that is pulling fathers apart from their families. Nothing is more important for our children or for our future as a nation.

NOTES

1. New York Times, September 25, 1986, C7.
2. D. B. Rutman and A. H. Rutman, *A Place in Time: Middlesex County, Virginia, 1650-1750* (New York: Norton, 1984).
3. Sara McLanahan and Gary Sandefur, *Growing Up With a Single Parent* (Cambridge, MA: Harvard University Press, 1994), 67-68.
4. Lawrence Stone, "The Road to Polygamy," *New York Review of Books*, March 2, 1989, 14.
5. Judith A. Seltzer, "Relationships Between Fathers and Children Who Live Apart: The Father's Role After Separation," *Journal of Marriage and the Family* 53 (1991): 79-101.
6. Frank Furstenberg, Jr., and Christine W. Nord, "Parenting Apart: Patterns of Childbearing After Marital Disruption," *Journal of Marriage and the Family* 47 (1985):893-905; Frank Furstenberg, Jr., Christine W. Nord, James L. Peterson, and Nicholas Zill, "The Life Course of Children of Divorce: Marital Disruption and Parental Contact." *American Sociological Review* 48 (1983):656-658.
7. For a popular introduction to the new field of evolutionary psychology, see Robert Wright, *The Moral Animal* (New York: Vintage Books, 1994).
8. Data sources can be found in chapter two of David Popenoe, *Life Without Father* (New York: Free Press, 1996).

9. Judith Seltzer, "Consequences of Marital Dissolution for Children." *Annual Review of Sociology* 20 (1994):235-266 (esp. 244).

10. Terry Lugaila, *Households, Families and Children: A Thirty-Year Perspective.* Current Population Reports P23-181 (Washington, DC: U.S. Bureau of the Census, 1992).

11. Irwin Garfinkel and Sara S. McLanahan, *Single Mothers and Their Children: A New American Dilemma* (Washington, DC: Urban Institute, 1986).

12. McLanahan and Sandefur, *Growing Up With a Single Parent.*

13. Barbara Dafoe Whitehead, *The Divorce Culture.* (New York: Alfred A. Knopf, 1997).

14. Data sources can be found in Popenoe, *Life Without Father,* Chap. 5.

15. John Snarey, *How Fathers Care for the Next Generation* (Cambridge, MA: Harvard University Press, 1993), 35-36.

16. Nancy A. Crowell and Ethel M. Leeper (eds.) *America's Fathers and Public Policy* (Washington, DC: National Academy Press, 1994), 8.

17. Reported in Kim A. McDonald, "The Secrets of Animal Play." *Chronicle of Higher Education,* July 13, 1995, A9-A13.

18. E. Greenberger, "Defining Psychosocial Maturity in Adolescence," in P. Karoly and J. J. Steffen (eds.), *Adolescent Behavior Disorders: Foundation and Contemporary Concerns* (Lexington, MA: D. C. Heath, 1984), 3-39.

19. The evidence is reviewed in Popenoe, *Life Without Father,* Chaps. 2 and 5.

20. Data provided by the National Fatherhood Initiative, Gaithersburg, MD.

21. Kathleen E. Kiernan, "The Impact of Family Disruptions in Childhood on Transitions Made in Young Adult Life," *Population Studies* 46 (1992):213-234.

22. The evidence is reviewed in Popenoe, *Life Without Father,* Chap. 2.

23. See David Finkelhor, "Current Information on the Scope and Nature of Child Sexual Abuse," *Future of Children* 4 (1994): no. 2, 31-53.

24. David T. Courtwright, *Violent Land: Single Men and Social Disorder from the Frontier to the Inner City* (Cambridge, MA: Harvard University Press, 1996).

25. Carolyn Pape Cowan and P. A. Cowan, "Men's Involvement in Parenthood: Identifying the Antecedents and Understanding the Barriers," in P. W. Berman and F. A. Pedersen (eds.) *Men's Transitions to Parenthood: Longitudinal Studies of Early Family Experience* Hillsdale, NJ: Lawrence Erlbaum, 1987), 145-174. See also C. P. Cowan and P. A. Cowan, *When Partners Become Parents* (New York: Basic Books, 1992).

26. D. H. Heath, "What Meaning and Effects Does Fatherhood Have for the Maturing of Professional Men?" *Merrill-Palmer Quarterly* 24, no. 2 (1978):265-278. See also D. H. Heath and H. E. Heath, *Fulfilling Lives: Paths to Maturity and Success* (San Francisco: Jossey-Bass, 1991).

27. Reported in *U. S. News & World Report,* February 27, 1995, 45.

28. Robert H. Coombs, "Marital Status and Personal Well-Being: A Literature Review," *Family Relations* 40 (1991):97-102; Walter R. Gove, C. B. Style and M. Hughes, "The Effect of Marriage on the Well-Being of Adults," *Journal of Family Issues* 11, no. 1 (1990):4-35; Arne Mastekaasa, "Marriage and

Psychological Well-Being: Some Evidence on Selection into Marriage" *Journal of Marriage and the Family* 54 (1992):901-911; Linda J. Waite, "Does Marriage Matter?" *Demography* 32, no.4 (1995):483-507.

29. Marianne W. Zawitz et al., "Highlights from Twenty Years of Surveying Crime Victims" (Washington, DC: Bureau of Justice Statistics,1993).

30. Ronet Bachman, *Violence Against Women* (Washington, DC: Bureau of Justice Statistics, 1994), 6.

31. Caroline Wolf Harlow, *Female Victims of Violent Crime* (Washington, DC: Bureau of Justice Statistics, 1991), 6.

THREE

DADA-ISM IN THE 1990S:
GETTING PAST BABY TALK ABOUT FATHERLESSNESS

Judith Stacey

IN THE YOUTHFUL YEARS OF THE TWENTIETH CENTURY, a self-consciously dissident group of Western artists generated a movement that, in the words of my desktop dictionary: "flouted conventional aesthetic and cultural values by producing works marked by nonsense, travesty and incongruity. Dada, of baby-talk origin."[1] Now, as the century expires, self-consciously mainstream politicians in the United States actively compete for prominence in a rather different sort of dada-ist movement. The products of this movement also display a good deal of nonsense, travesty, and incongruity, but contemporary dada-ism proudly flaunts, rather than flouts, conventional cultural values.

Late-millennial dada-ism is an increasingly prominent thematic trend within the peculiar politics of family values in the United States. During the 1990s, as family values discourse became ever more ubiquitous on the national political landscape, its central rhetorical focus began to shift from laments over the social hazards unleashed by miscreant moms to those caused by missing dads. Contemporary dada-ism blossoms in a plethora of voices that decry a cultural epidemic of "milkbox dads." Across a broad ideological and cultural spectrum, men have been mobilizing in the name of the father—among them, the mythopoetic men's quest to commune with paternal spirits in the wilderness sparked by Robert Bly; fathers' rights groups contesting for child custody; the Christian Promise Keepers movement crowding massive sports stadiums with men hugging, praying, and testifying; the African American Million Man March called by Louis Farrakhan in October 1995; the National Center for Fathering founded by Ken Canfield; and the National Fatherhood Initiative which David Blankenhorn spearheaded in concert with an aggressive promotional campaign for his book, *Fatherless America*.[2]

Indeed, dada-ist literature is all the rage. One year after Blankenhorn's *Fatherless America* appeared, David Popenoe, his colleague at the Institute for American Values and a former coauthor, published *Life Without Father*, a book that differs more in tone than substance from Blankenhorn's overwrought one. Even former Vice-President Dan Quayle has ventured into this popular branch of family sociology. During the 1996 electoral season, Quayle published *The American Family*, a book of five "case studies" of contemporary families. The title of the opening chapter applauds "The New Consensus" that now putatively pertains in the sociological field. "America has reached a new consensus," the book begins, "on the importance of the traditional family—a consensus unthinkable just a few years ago."[3] Quayle claims that from "all points on the political spectrum, from Bill Clinton to Bill Bennett"—a rather narrow spectrum, one might note, that excludes me and perhaps many readers as well—a national consensus has now been achieved on the validity of his once-infamous Murphy Brown speech: "Fathers *do* matter. Families *are* the basis of our society. We *must* support the unified model of father, mother, and child."[4]

Even Harlequin romance novel industry moguls now stake profit margins on appeals to women desperately seeking daddies for their children. The most popular book series that Harlequin Enterprises Ltd. currently publishes have names like *Fabulous Fathers, Family Man, Bundles of Joy,* and *Hometown Reunion.* "He's the 1990s hero of the billion-dollar romance novel industry," according to a recent Associated Press report, "a man for whom children and family come first." This "transformation of romance heroes from heartless playboys or intimidating studs into nurturing—but still hunky—daddies has come about mostly in response to readers." [5]

These days the kind of men such readers seek might be found reading articles like "Breakfast for Mom: The Way to Her Heart," or "A Capital Dad: Reflections on Fatherhood from Vice-President Al Gore" in new market niche magazines like *Modern Dad: For a New Generation of Fathers.*[6] Or perhaps they are logging onto the Internet, where paternal advice, support, and chat groups, such as "Fathernet," now flourish. They might even be digesting stories like "The Men Who Clean Toilets and the Women Who Love Them" in "At-Home Dad," a quarterly newsletter that Peter Baylies founded in 1994, two years after Digital had laid him off and launched him into his full-time father career. The newsletter depicts itself as "devoted to providing connections and resources for the 2 million fathers who stay home with their children."[7] Meanwhile, politicians, scholars, and activists busily convene conferences on the subject, such as the lively, analytical one on "the politics of fatherlessness" held at Rutgers University in May 1996, which generated this volume, or the more alarmist, ideological one sponsored by Blankenhorn's Institute for American Values and the National Fatherhood Initiative, "The Fatherhood Movement: A Call to Action," that took place at the University of Minnesota a few months later.[8] It is not surprising, therefore, that the public seems to be absorbing the message. In a 1996 Gallup Poll, 79 percent of those surveyed agreed with the statement: "The most significant family or social problem facing America is the physical absence of the father from the home."[9]

MOM AND POP CHARTS

These recent developments all index the subtle shift in family values campaigns' public spotlight focus from the politics of motherhood to the politics of fatherhood. Or, to be more precise, national rhetoric has been shifting from an emphasis on the dangers of a motherless society to that of a fatherless society. Of course, a shift is not synonymous with a substitution. Certainly, discourses lamenting maternal sins of commission and omission continue to thrive in the 1990s—be they to excoriate teen moms and "welfare queens" for irresponsibility and dependency, to condemn single, career women like "Murphy Brown" who selfishly dare to mother outside of marriage, or even to rebuke married career women like Hillary Clinton who fail to conceal their greater commitments to public than to private domestic work. However, public conversations about paternal crisis now compete for, and frequently usurp, center stage. Whether the "two-parent family is an endangered species," as many pundits claim, there is no question that two parental crises discourses are flourishing in tandem.[10]

Political campaigns conducted in the name of The Family are now in their third decade in the United States. "Pro-family" movements erupted into public visibility during the middle of the 1970s, initially as an explicit backlash against the sexual revolution, the counterculture, feminism, and gay liberation, all of which were viewed (and not without cause) as a threat to prevailing definitions of family and motherhood. The politics of motherhood were central to this early, primarily evangelical Christian campaign by the "New Right." New Right pro-family leaders like Jerry Falwell and Phyllis Schlafly targeted feminists in particular for abandoning domesticity in what they portrayed as a selfish, individualistic quest for careers and sexual gratification. Maternal neglect became a favorite trope in New Right rhetoric, which represented working moms and day care as endangering the health and welfare of their children and country.[11] The antiabortion wing of the pro-family movement capsulized, and capitalized on, pervasive cultural anxieties over the rapidly eroding status and feasibility of full-time motherhood. Contemporaneous challenges by women to the double standard of sexual morality exacerbated these fears, as feminist scholars have demonstrated.[12]

Viewed in this historical context, the contemporary politics of fatherlessness represents a double discursive shift—first, from gender to broadly understood family politics, and second, from a mother to a father fixation within the domain of family politics. Moreover, whereas the sources and rhetoric of the family values crusades of the 1970s and early 1980s were almost exclusively right wing and primarily religious, by the late 1980s, family values discourses began to proliferate and diversify across a remarkably broad ideological spectrum. Currently this terrain extends not only to the left-leaning "politics of meaning" promoted by Michael Lerner, founder and editor of *Tikkun,* but also to the now-flourishing arena of gay pro-family politics.[13] Within this cultural landscape, contemporary preoccupation with fatherhood and fatherlessness represents, in part, a displaced postfeminist discourse on gender.

At first glance, this might strike many feminists and mothers as good news. Isn't it about time that Dad shared the heat with Mom for the imagined evils of changing family forms? Certainly many feminists long have called and struggled for renovating dated, and oppressive, definitions of fatherhood and masculinity. Later I will assess this progressive potential of the politics of fatherlessness. Nonetheless, feminists have excellent reasons to remain skeptical about the popularity of 1990s dada-ist fashions, because too often these still blame women, and often feminism, for precipitating fatherlessness. Much talk about fatherlessness portrays feminism as leading women selfishly to deny children the benefits of paternal investment—by choosing to have children outside of marriage and even outside of heterosexual coupling; by deserting or ejecting husbands and fathers they deem unsatisfactory and then taking unfair advantage of maternal child custody preferences; or, alternatively, by driving men away from marriage and paternity through the unreasonable, excessive demand that men embrace a "new fatherhood" whose responsibilities strike many as uncomfortably similar to those of motherhood.

In fact, some contemporary dada-ist outpourings are quite explicitly restorationist in their desire to reestablish rigid gender codes for parenting and to elevate paternal over maternal authority. The rhetoric of both the Promise Keepers movement and the Million Man March contain elements of this nostalgia for paternal family headship. For example, a Promise Keepers treatise urges each of its members to "sit down with your wife and say something like this: 'Honey, I've made a terrible mistake. I've given you my role. I gave up leading this family, and I forced you to take my place. Now I must reclaim that role.' I'm not suggesting you *ask* for your role back, I'm urging you to *take* it back. [T]here can be no compromise here. If you're going to lead, you must lead. Treat the lady gently and lovingly. But *lead!*"[14] But so, too, does the rhetoric of many who claim the mantle of social science as authority for their views. For example, appearing on The Jim Lehrer News Hour the Monday after Father's Day in 1996, Wade Horn, a member of the Council on Families in America, identified fatherlessness as the nation's most urgent crisis: "It's not one of many national crises. It is *the* national crisis, because it drives everything else."[15] Horn proceeded to echo sentiments he had expressed in print the previous year: "Reversing the trend toward fatherlessness will not be easy. To do so, we will have to embrace some unpopular ideas. The first is that fathers make unique and irreplaceable contributions to the lives of their children. Unique means that they provide something different from mothers; they are not simply part-time mommy substitutes. Irreplaceable means that when they are absent, children suffer."[16]

Blankenhorn has become one of the most overtly nostalgic, and inflammatory, chauvinists among today's secular dada-ist preachers. In *Fatherless America,* he scornfully rejects the "New Father ideal" that many feminists, and now Harlequin romance novelists, affirm:

> The New Father model does not merely unburden men of breadwinning as a special obligation. Ultimately, it unburdens them of fatherhood itself. For, as the example of breadwinning demonstrates, the essence of the New Father model is a repudiation of gendered social roles. But fatherhood, by definition, is a gendered social role. To ungender fatherhood—to deny males any gender-based role in family life—is to deny fatherhood as a social activity. What remains may be New. But there is no more Father.[17]

As Blankenhorn's prose reveals, a great deal of contemporary lament about fatherlessness indirectly expresses profound male gender anxiety about the erosion of received definitions of masculinity, and particularly fear of emasculation. In his chapter entitled "The New Father," Blankenhorn derisively titles the section immediately following the lines I just quoted "Why Can't a Man Be More Like a Woman?"[18] There he indulges in a kind of 1990s postfeminist hostility toward women and motherhood with resonances of the assault on "momism" in the 1940s and 1950s catalyzed by the publication of Phillip Wylie's *Generation of Vipers.*[19] In that phenomenal best-seller, Wylie coined "momism" as a term of opprobrium to alert his fellow country*men* to the dangers of a midcentury masculinity crisis. Like Blankenhorn, Wylie worried about myriad evils deriving from the feminization of American families. Ironically enough, however, in Wylie's view, full-time motherhood was the source of this threat. In overheated, almost hysterical prose, he argued that an army of overprotective, shallow, frustrated women with excessive, vicarious investments in their children, and particularly in their sons, were producing a vulnerable nation of sissies incapable of independent thought or courageous action:

> "Her boy," having been "protected" by her love, and carefully, even shudderingly, shielded from his logical development through his barbaric period, or childhood (so that he has either to become a barbarian as a man or else to spend most of his energy denying the barbarism that howls in his brain—an autonomous remnant of the youth he was forbidden), is cushioned against any major step in his progress toward maturity. Mom steals from the generation of women behind her (which she has, as a still further defense, also sterilized of integrity and courage) that part of her boy's personality which should have become the love of a female contemporary. Mom transmutes it into sentimentality for herself.[20]

In other words, Wylie construed the very breadwinner-homemaker family whose decline dada-ists like Blankenhorn blame for social decay as itself the prime threat to men's virility, national strength, and even the very future of democracy. In his extensive annotations to the second edition of *Generation of Vipers* in 1955, Wylie went so far as to blame momism for the capitulation of captured U.S. soldiers to North Korean Communist indoctrination (and even for McCarthyism itself!): "'McCarthyism,' the rule of unreason, is one with momism: a noble end aborted by sick-minded means, a righteous intent—in terrorism fouled and tyranny foundered."[21]

Whereas Blankenhorn, looking backward, nostalgically applauds the beneficial ministrations of full-time mothers and extols male breadwinning as nearly synonymous with masculinity and paternity, during the heyday of this division of labor Wylie judged it "as invidious a spiritual parasitism as any in the book."[22] His book tried to arouse the exploited, henpecked masses to rebel: "We must face the dynasty of the dames at once, deprive them of our pocketbooks when they waste the substance in them, and take back our dreams which, without the perfidious materialism of mom, were shaping up a new and braver world. We must drive roads to Rio and to Moscow and stop spending all our strength in the manufacture of girdles: it is time that mom's sag became known to the desperate public."[23]

If 1990s dada-ism echoes momism in its anxiety over the effects of feminized child-rearing on boys, the manifest content of the anxiety is nearly the opposite. Today's dada-ists worry more about the production of criminals than of cowards, of hyper- and lethal forms of masculinity rather than effeminacy. The crusade to combat fatherlessness feeds on fears that it generates lawlessness, recklessness, and, ultimately, barbarism. Characteristic of this pitch is an alarmist selection of correlational data that psychologist David Lykken published in the *Chronicle of Higher Education*: "In the United States among boys aged 12 to 17, the percentage who are arrested for violent crime has doubled in the past 15 years. Not coincidentally, the percentage of children under 18 who are being reared without fathers also has doubled during this period. Nationally, about 70 percent of school dropouts, 70 percent of teenage girls who are pregnant and unmarried, and 70 percent of incarcerated juvenile delinquents were raised without fathers."[24] Lykken cited Blankenhorn (*Fatherless America*) as a key source for some of this data and in support of the rather "reckless" interpretations that both of them draw: "Fatherlessness is the most harmful demographic trend of this generation. It is the leading cause of declining child well-being in our society. It is also the engine driving our most urgent social problems from crime to adolescent pregnancy to child sexual abuse to domestic violence against women."[25] David Popenoe provides a uniquely dada-ist variation on this theme in an article in the *Utne Reader*. Immediately after quoting a claim from the right-wing Family Research Council that fathers "give children practice in regulating their own emotions and recognizing others' emotional clues," Popenoe appends as a stunning non sequitur this remarkably uninformative statistic: "A study of convicted murderers in Texas found that 90 percent of them either didn't play as children or played abnormally."[26]

The claim that fatherlessness leads to lawlessness has become so ubiquitous that it is approaching the status of national dogma. Even *It Takes a Village,* Hillary Clinton's putatively liberal defense of child welfare, succumbs to its doctrine. The First Lady approvingly cites Daniel Patrick Moynihan's warning that "the absence of fathers in the lives of children—especially boys—leads to increased rates of violence and aggressiveness, as well as a general loss of the civilizing influence marriage and responsible parenthood historically provide any society."[27] Moynihan first issued this warning in the mid-1960s in his now-immortalized, controversial critique of a "tangle of pathology" he perceived in the rapidly rising rates of fatherless African American families.[28] Viewed in this context, 1990s dada-ism is not only a postfeminist echo of 1950s "momism" but also a latter-day, white-faced coda of Moynihan's 1960s attack on "Black matriarchy."

RESTORATIONIST INFLUENCES

Dada-ism in the 1990s is an arena of cultural politics worth taking very seriously, because it has been coloring a broad canvas of reactionary politics. In some cases, the links are explicit or obvious. For example, dada-ists have cited the risks of fatherlessness in recent campaigns to repeal no-fault divorce laws and even to support the instituting of rather extreme restrictions on divorce. More blatantly dada-ist is the burgeoning popularity of federal and state demands for mandatory identification at birth of every child's biological paternity. Although many feminists sympathize with such efforts to hold men responsible for all the children they sire, I believe that the principal effects of these requirements will cause women and children much greater harm than benefit. First, they cement a rigid biological definition of parenthood, which most feminists have prudently challenged. Moreover, they are far more likely to strengthen paternal rights that can conflict with the interests of women and children—such as the right to prevent an abortion or to contest for custody—than they are to foster paternal responsibility or cooperation in caretaking. In the widely publicized Baby Richard case, for example, a biological father won a custody struggle against adoptive parents who had raised a three-year-old since infancy, because he had not known of the baby's birth or consented to the adoption. Two years after winning custody, the father separated from his wife, the biological mother, and left the son she had given up for adoption in her custody.[29]

Similarly, some dada-ists directly call for restricting access to sperm and fertility services to heterosexual, married couples. Blankenhorn, for example, scathingly condemns procreation by lesbians or unmarried heterosexual women through donor insemination: "State legislatures across the nation should support fatherhood by regulating sperm banks. New laws should prohibit sperm banks and others from selling sperm to unmarried women and limit the use of artificial insemination to cases of married couples experiencing fertility problems. In a good society, people do not traffic commercially in the production of radically fatherless children."[30] Soon after the publication of *Fatherless America,* mainstream journalists began to embrace and disseminate Blankenhorn's views. "Promoting No-Dad Families," an article which appeared in *U.S. News & World Report,* for example, cited Blankenhorn as authority for the claim that: "The consensus of studies is that no-father children, as a group, are at risk in all races and at all income levels. If so, doesn't society have a stake in discouraging the intentional creation of fatherless children?"[31] Similar concerns have appeared in even ostensibly more liberal publications, such as the *Atlantic Monthly.*[32]

Some of the reactionary political effects of dada-ism are more indirect but also more profound. Erosion of a social safety net for our most vulnerable families likely will prove to be the most consequential casualty. Indeed, the preamble to the welfare reform bill of 1996 explicitly justified the draconian measures it was about to enact in a dada-ist simulation of social science rhetoric. "The Congress makes the following *findings*" (emphasis added), the bill announces and then proceeds to itemize a peculiar array of dada-ist assertions in defense of its actions, such as

(1) Marriage is the foundation of a successful society.

(2) Marriage is an essential institution of a successful society that promotes the interests of children.

(3) Promotion of responsible fatherhood and motherhood is integral to successful child rearing and the well-being of children. . . .

(7) The negative consequences of an out-of-wedlock birth on the mother, the child, the family and society are *well documented* as follows. . . .

What follows are six misleading generalizations about these consequences, including claims that out-of-wedlock children are more likely to suffer child abuse, low cognitive attainment, and lower educational aspirations. The eighth of the enumerated assertions goes even further by warning that "the negative consequences of raising children in single-parent homes are *well documented*," and then listing thirteen harmful effects. Several of these expose the dada-ist gender presumptions of the Congress, because they equate single-parent with fatherless families. For example, one of the identified dangers of single-parent *families* is that "the absence of a *father* in the life of a child has a negative effect on school performance and peer adjustment" (emphasis added).[33]

Paradoxically, and somewhat poignantly, Senator Moynihan is the now-legendary forefather of the very dada-ist ideology embedded in the Welfare Reform Act of 1996, which, to his credit, he bitterly and eloquently opposed in the end.[34] Yet as recently as

1994, Moynihan was still fueling dada-ist fervor in a fund-raising appeal letter which reprinted an alarmist warning about the evils of fatherlessness he had issued thirty years earlier:

> From the wild Irish slums of the 19th-century Eastern seaboard to the riot-torn suburbs of Los Angeles, there is one unmistakable lesson in American history: a community that allows a large number of young men to grow up in broken families, dominated by women, never acquiring any stable relationship to male authority, never acquiring any set of rational expectations about the future—that community asks for and gets chaos. Crime, violence, unrest, unrestrained lashing out at the whole social structure—that is not only to be expected; it is very near to inevitable.[35]

As noted earlier, the First Lady herself embraced Moynihan as authority for similar views. More tragically, the welfare reform bill whose name Moynihan correctly termed "Orwellian"[36] explicitly justified its actions with the very same convictions.

Thus, the social and political products of the contemporary dada-ist movement are far-reaching and, in my view, deeply destructive, even when evaluated within their own terms. Not only do they deflect attention from the underlying social sources of "fatherlessness," but worse, they help to legitimate active withdrawal of urgently necessary social responses to the needs of "fatherless" children and their beleaguered caretakers. In these ways they unwittingly harm the very populations they purport to help.

BACK TO THE DRAWING BOARDS

Anyone genuinely committed to the best interests of children, their caretakers, and the world we all now inhabit has good cause to reject the current fashion of dada-ist baby talk about fatherlessness and to foster more constructive public discourse on fatherhood. To that end, in the remaining pages I want first to disrupt dada-ist claims that social science researchers have reached a consensus that fatherlessness has harmful effects on children. Next, I suggest why dada-ist social science fosters policies doomed either to fail or to cause more harm than good even to their intended beneficiaries. Finally, I nonetheless want to take seriously the social problem not of fatherless families but of what historian John Gillis has cogently termed "family-less fathers."[37] This, of course, is the daunting problem of redefining outmoded, and therefore often disturbing, masculinities to meet the gender, family, and economic challenges of increasingly global postmodern conditions.

Let us begin with the recurrent dada-ist claim that social scientists have achieved a consensus on the dangers of fatherlessness. Stated baldly, the claim is categorically false. Categorically false in quite a literal sense. For quite apart from the status of pertinent research on the subject, the very category "fatherlessness" itself would never pass social scientific muster. It is far too broad and murky a concept to use in conducting or reporting meaningful social science research. One shouldn't need a social science degree to recognize that there are quite a few radically distinct varieties of "fatherless" family structures, each of which implies rather different social and psychological circumstances for children. Some children lose a father through death, others after parents divorce or separate, although it is important to remember that parental divorce or separation does not necessarily result in fatherless families. Some children, on the other hand, do not live with a father to begin with, if ever. In fact, the Census Bureau counts nearly all children born to unmarried women as members of single-mother families, although this category is also quite diverse. Some single-mother families originate from unintended pregnancies or after men abandon women during wanted pregnancies. Some unmarried women, however, quite actively, even desperately, seek to become pregnant or to adopt or foster children. They become mothers in a variety of ways that may or may not involve the active participation of biological or social fathers, or other mothers, not to speak of a range of additional given and chosen kin.

TV sitcom heroine Murphy Brown, of course, became the national icon of chosen single motherhood during the 1992 presidential election campaign when Dan Quayle branded her an immoral, "cultural elite" role model.[38] This is rather ironic, because the sitcom anchorwoman did not actively choose to become pregnant; she merely chose not to terminate a pregnancy conceived during a nostalgic fling with her former husband. Increasing numbers of unmarried women, however, have indeed aggressively pursued motherhood, or "radical fatherlessness," to use Blankenhorn's provocative term. But this, too, is a heterogeneous family category. Many are single heterosexual women, like Murphy Brown; but unlike Murphy, many actively seek to conceive through heterosexual intercourse fully intending to parent without the biological father. Others choose to adopt children through either domestic or international sources, while increasing numbers of single women have been conceiving through donor insemination arranged via personal networks, private physicians, or sperm banks. Lesbians represent a growing segment of contemporary women choosing to become mothers outside of heterosexual marriage, but their planned parenthood strategies and family patterns are even more diverse than among unmarried heterosexuals. Increasing numbers of lesbian couples plan for and rear children in what are actually socially invisible, two-parent families. Frequently, lesbian mothers parent within more complex kin arrangements that sometimes include biological fathers or other men. A teenage daughter from one quite creative, successful lesbian family of my acquaintance who frequently speaks publicly on behalf of COLAGE (Children of Lesbians and Gays Everywhere) has been parented by four moms and currently resides with two of these and her younger, nonbiological brother.[39]

For social scientists to achieve consensus concerning disproportionate risks and harms derived from fatherlessness, research would have to demonstrate that children living in all of these very different kinds of families are more apt to be inadequately parented than are children in comparable, conventional, heterosexual married-couple families. Yet social science research on family structure demonstrates nothing of the kind. In fact, systematic, comparative research on the many diverse forms of fatherlessness scarcely exists. Dada-ists who decry the destructiveness of fatherlessness typically conflate and misconstrue research literature on at least three quite distinct species of "fatherless" families—those produced through divorce; through unwed, and generally youthful, single motherhood; and through intentional, typically more mature, lesbian parenthood. Even so, no consensus, but lively debate, characterizes contemporary social scientific discourse on the sources and/or effects of all three routes to "fatherlessness."

Currently, the predominant (but by no means universal) view prevailing among family scholars is that *all other things being equal,* two-parent families generally are preferable to one-parent families. Of course, in real life, all "other" things are almost never equal, and the most careful studies and the most careful researchers confirm what most of us know from our own lives: The quality of any family's relationships and resources readily trumps its formal structure or form. Access to economic, educational, and social resources; the quality and consistency of parental nurturance, guidance, and responsibility; and the degree of domestic harmony, conflict, and hostility affect child development and welfare *far* more substantially than does the particular number, gender, sexual orientation, and marital status of parents or the family structure in which children are reared.

Take, for example, contemporary dada-ist preoccupation with the damaging effects of divorce on children. This is the central theme of Whitehead's recent book, *The Divorce Culture,* which her colleague at the Institute for American Values, Maggie Gallagher, wholeheartedly endorses. "The academic evidence—that children raised in broken homes are on average poorer, sicker, unhappier, less successful in school, at work, in relationships (even when income is held constant)—is chilling enough," Gallagher proclaims.[40] In fact, however, scholars actively disagree over whether divorce in and of itself harms children. It is true that currently, most mainstream family scholars subscribe to the view that parental divorce places children at higher levels of risk for a variety of emotional, social, and economic difficulties than does an "intact" marriage. A recent, particularly comprehensive study of divorce concludes, for example, that "children of divorce are at least twice as likely as those from intact families to display the problems included in our study (delinquency, early sexual intercourse, emotional distress, and academic difficulties)."[41] At first glance, this statement seems to sustain the veracity of alarmist dada-ist claims, like Whitehead's and Gallagher's. Reputable social science, however, like reputable scholarship, generally demands much more than a first glance. In this case, even a casual second glimpse at the literature is sufficient to challenge the overly hasty causal inferences about the damaging consequences of divorce that dada-ists draw.

To begin with, even if divorce can be said to double the developmental risks that children face, the actual rate of risk remains low, as Ronald Simons and his associates, the researchers in the study just quoted, quickly underscore:

> Children of divorce are not a homogeneous group that inevitably develops problems. As our findings and those of others make clear, there is great variability among children whose parents divorce, and *most* children of divorce do not develop long-term difficulties in functioning. And, a child is not immune to problems simply because he or she lives with two parents. A significant proportion of children living with both parents develops psychosocial problems [emphasis added].[42]

Similarly, testifying before Congress in 1996, Andrew Cherlin, a leading family researcher, warned policymakers that the effects of divorce on children often are exaggerated. Cherlin succinctly distilled the essence of this body of social science research in plain speech: "Divorce is not harmless, but most kids are not seriously harmed by divorce in the long-term."[43]

Taking yet a third glance at the research weakens even this modest claim about the injurious effects of divorce, because it reveals that at most only a very small proportion of what quantitative social scientists call "the variance" in measures that differentiate children from divorced and "intact" families can be attributed to the structural factor of divorce itself. Most of the harms that divorce appears to inflict on children derive not from subsequent "fatherlessness" but from negative circumstances that too often precede or follow a divorce—most significantly, parental hostility, parental stress, and economic decline. In a particularly careful and judicious summary of this research, Janet Johnston explains: "Exposure to parental conflict, together with affective distress and psychological disorders within parents (usually the caretaking mother), is a greater hazard to children than are many other stressful events associated with divorce, including acute loss due to separation from a parent (usually the father)."[44]

Divorcing parents certainly "enjoy" no monopoly on parental conflict, psychic distress, or disorder, although they likely suffer from these somewhat more than do other parents. However, research indicates that children exposed to a high-conflict marriage generally fare worse than those whose parents manage to negotiate a relatively low-conflict divorce.[45] Indeed, there is a clear consensus among family scholars that the risks to children of parental hostilities utterly overshadow the risks of divorce and that parental conflict actually accounts for a great deal of the reported correlations between divorce and adverse outcomes. Moreover, Gallagher's claim that "academic evidence" shows that the damaging effects of divorce remain "even when income is held constant" actually inverts the predominant view held by mainstream analysts of divorce research. There is a clear consensus among family scholars that the hazards to children of parental divorce absolutely pale in comparison to those of parental poverty, unemployment, and income decline. As Simons and coauthors summarize: "Much of the association between family structure and parenting practices is mediated by economic pressure, negative events, and depression."[46] Thus, as they explain, "in large measure, the relationship between parental divorce and adolescent problems is explained by the following causal sequence: Marital disruption increases the probability that a woman will experience economic pressures, negative life events, and psychological depression. This strain and emotional distress tend to reduce the quality of her parenting. Reductions in quality of parenting, in turn, increase a child's risk for emotional and behavioral problems."[47]

Finally, divorce is no more monolithic a phenomenon than any other family experience. Indeed, for a growing minority of children, divorce actually brings greater contact and involvement with their fathers. After all, increasing numbers of divorced men are assuming primary or joint custody of children with whom they often spent far less time before—a fashionable theme in popular culture ever since the film *Kramer vs. Kramer* attracted throngs in the mid-1980s. On the other hand, a parental divorce clearly liberates some children, as well as adults, from deeply destructive relationships. Indeed, for a significant minority of children, divorce ushers in a form of "fatherlessness" that provides welcome relief. I do not present these challenges to the doomsday divorce chorus in order "to fight the notion that marriage matters," as Gallagher has mistakenly claimed.[48] Rather, I do so to fight the notion that only one form of family matters, or that it is superior to all other forms for all children, all adults, and society as a whole. On the contrary, what matters most is the character and quality of relationships, of parenthood, and of the conditions in which these occur, whether parents decide to marry or divorce. Neither marriage nor fatherhood, in and of itself, protects children, not even from the risks of "fatherlessness."

Quite similar distinctions, findings, and complexities apply to research on the second widespread genre of "fatherlessness"—children born to unwed mothers. Unsurprisingly, children reared by highly educated, comparatively affluent unwed mothers typically fare far better emotionally, economically, educationally, and socially than those reared by two married parents who have lesser educational and economic resources.[49] Of course, few women choose to become unwed mothers because they actively wish to parent alone. Rather, most single mothers, like Murphy Brown and like Shoshana Alexander, author of *In Praise of Single Parents*, actively wish to become mothers but fail to find acceptable male partners willing and able to share the responsibilities and rewards of rearing children.[50] No one I know, least of all a single mother, would deny that it is demanding to parent alone, more demanding than it is to share parenting with a cooperative, responsible second parent. The issues in dispute, however, are how to identify the character of the special burdens single mothers bear and, thus, how best to alleviate them.

Dada-ists claim the problem is "fatherlessness" and respond by further stigmatizing and marginalizing single-mother families. Most social science evidence, like common sense, however, suggests that the chief handicaps unwed mothers face are deficits of time, money, and social support—deficits for which there are much better social remedies than moral opprobrium. In any case, there is little or no evidence that what the children of single mothers need most is the addition of a *male* parent. In fact, a recent study found that children reared by single mothers were nearly as successful as those reared in conventional two-parent homes and *more* successful than children reared in households headed by a single father.[51] Moreover, one can state categorically that there is *no research support whatsoever* to substantiate dada-ist objections to the third genre of fatherless families—lesbian-couple families. Although this body of research is comparatively young—like the family form itself—thus far, not a single study of lesbian parents has found their children to be less successful than, or even particularly different from, children reared by heterosexual parents.[52] The primary burden of "fatherlessness" that these children suffer derives from legal discrimination and social prejudice against their families, a burden that contemporary dada-ism only serves to heighten. In my view, the pertinent research demonstrates that fathers indeed *are* expendable, but so, too, are mothers. What are not expendable are caring, responsible *parents* of any gender, or a responsible and responsive society.

DADA-IST DAMAGE CONTROL

Paradoxically, dada-ist belief in the destructive effects of fatherlessness has destructive effects itself. For, as I indicated earlier, dada-ist ideology has fueled reactionary policy and cultural initiatives that are demonstrably injurious to vast numbers of children and families and, in my view, to our social fabric more generally. Dada-ism fosters support for knee-jerk family values, quick fixes which are futile at best and more likely to backfire or worse. What if one believed (as I do not) that one family form is superior and that every child should have a "right" to have a father? (Interestingly, dada-ists rarely seem to concern themselves with whether a child also has a right to a mother. The growing phenomenon of single-father families seems to inspire few laments.) Even if one wished to combat "fatherlessness," what could be done that would do "fatherless" children and their parents more good than harm? Very few policy derivatives of dada-ism seem promising here, because while one cannot mandate or legislate the quality of intimate relationships, misguided policies can readily make them worse.

For example, the case against "divorce culture" made by critics like Whitehead and Gallagher has encouraged more than twenty states to consider legislation to repeal no-fault divorce in cases involving children. Yet reinstituting fault criteria into divorce proceedings poses even greater dangers to women and children. Ironically enough, in a *New York Times* op-ed, Whitehead herself belatedly warned that "rather than alleviating the damage divorce does to mothers and children," repealing no-fault "will only make their situation worse." Indeed, as Whitehead points out, it will "intensify the pain of divorce for children. Nothing is more emotionally devastating to children than a prolonged conflict among their parents. Such friction will only worsen if parents fight over who is at fault in the breakup. The children will be caught in the crossfire."[53] Battered women would have to mount dangerous, and expensive, court battles against their abusers, while emotionally desperate spouses would find incentives to fabricate abuse, to forfeit economic support, or simply to desert. Moreover, the repeal of no-fault might easily have the ironic consequence of inducing many men, as well as women, to avoid legal marriage in the first place. It was experience with just these sorts of unintended consequences of prohibitions against divorce that led voters in the Roman Catholic Republic of Ireland to pass a constitutional amendment in 1995 to make divorce legal for the first time since the nation won its independence from England.

Likewise, dada-ist hostility to "fatherless" lesbian families helped to justify the Orwellian 1996 Defense of Marriage Act (in my view, better named the Offensive Marriage Act), the current rash of state-level campaigns to prevent the legalization of same-sex marriage, and related attempts to restrict child custody and adoption rights to married, heterosexual couples, such as an initiative proposed in California during the 1996 electoral season by Governor Pete Wilson. Of course, the most tangible effect of these assaults on the legitimacy of lesbian-parent families is to deny stability, legitimacy, resources, and respect to the millions of children who now live in what are often *invisible* two-parent homes. The legal invisibility of lesbian-couple families produces cruel and unnecessary tragedies. For example, when Kristin Pearlman's biological mother, a lesbian, died an early death, the youngster lost her beloved second parent as well, because a Florida court refused to recognize her surviving lesbian coparent as a legitimate relative. It took four years of traumatic separation and legal struggle to reunite this unnecessarily "broken family."[54] And legally sanctioned, dada-ist discrimination produces even greater outrages. In August 1996, for example, a Florida judge removed an eleven-year-old girl from the home of her lesbian mother and awarded custody to her biological father—a man who had been convicted of murdering his first wife in 1974—because the judge wanted "to give this girl a chance to live in a nonlesbian world."[55]

By far the most widespread tangible harm that contemporary dada-ism will inflict on real families derives from its contribution to welfare "reforms," which currently threaten millions of already impoverished "fatherless" children and their caretakers with homelessness, malnutrition, and devastation. Social scientists and politicians continue to debate the precise numbers of children and families who will fall victim to the severe new restrictions on eligibility for public assistance, but evidence is mounting that their ranks will be substantial. For example, a comprehensive study released by the Public Policy Institute of California in early 1997 found that one-fourth of families in our largest state now receive some form of public aid and that nearly half a million families, almost half of those who receive Aid to Families with Dependent Children, are "extremely vulnerable" to losing most or all of their income under the new welfare restrictions.[56] It is certainly difficult to imagine how such measures will introduce fathers or any other benefits into the perilous lives of children in such families.

In the end, however, it is difficult to believe that many dada-ists truly care about improving the actual lives of the members of most real "fatherless" families. Instead, the politics of fatherless-ness is a politics of displacement. Dada-ism functions as proxy rhetoric for antifeminist, antigay, xenophobic, and antiwelfare sentiments, which themselves displace direct engagement with the most fraught social divisions and anxieties in our nation. On the broadest level, contemporary dada-ism functions to deflect serious analysis and remedies away from the social sources of what are experienced and then reified as personal or familial problems. Thus, in *The American Family,* a book that promotes school vouchers, tax cuts, divorce restrictions, prayer in schools, and a full-scale conservative agenda, Dan Quayle dares to proclaim, "On this, we're all allies. *Strengthening families should not be a political issue.*"[57] Well, perhaps the former vice-president is right. Perhaps "we" could all agree that strengthening families *should* not be a political issue. However, we might just as readily endorse the goals of permanent peace on Earth and good will toward (and from) all men. Back here on imperfect planet Earth, however, there is no such thing as an apolitical platform for strengthening families, or even for agreeing on a definition for what constitutes the kind of family that we wish to strengthen.

In the current conservative, antigovernment, antitax and spending climate, dada-ism represents a profoundly political issue. By blaming massive global crises on individual moral failings and lapses of "personal responsibility," it rationalizes a sweeping privatization of resources and responsibility that social advocate Frances Fox Piven has characterized as a bald-faced redistribution of resources from the poor to the rich.[58]

Anyone with even cursory knowledge of the social science literature who genuinely wished to reduce fatherlessness and to strengthen most families would make it a political priority to provide secure employment and a living family wage to all workers, and most urgently to workers with less than a college education. After all, marriage rates rise and divorce rates fall as one goes up the income and employment ladder. Those particularly concerned about the declining ranks of ghetto fathers might try to redirect national priorities from building prisons to building schools and to reducing the spread of firearms. As the grim findings in a recent study by the Centers for Disease Control and Prevention demonstrate, the United States far exceeds the record of the twenty-six richest countries in the world in losing children to homicide, suicide, and deaths by firearms. Almost three out of four violent deaths of children in the industrialized world occur in the United States, and many more of the murder victims are boys.[59] Since dead boys do not grow up to become fathers, and since incarcerated, unemployed, and underemployed men comprise much of the expanding universe of milkbox dads, one might expect sincere dada-ists to address some of the most basic sources of the growing demographic imbalance between marriageable women and men in our nation's most impoverished communities. Instead, most dada-ists have proven uncharacteristically reticent about promoting the kind of rational, humane, and promising remedies for fatherless-ness that analysis of these data would suggest.

BRINGING UP DADA

Despite my passionate and stringent critique of dada-ism, I do not wish to dismiss all contemporary discussions of fatherlessness out of hand. Even a displaced discourse on the crises of contemporary masculinities is better than none at all. For this reason, I believe it would be a mistake if feminists and other progressives were to abdicate the arena of the politics of fatherlessness entirely. For, although fatherless families in and of themselves do not constitute a social problem, undomesticated men, as dada-ists such as Blan-kenhorn, Popenoe, and George Gilder like to point out (or "family-less fathers," in John Gillis's terms), often do seem to pose serious problems to themselves as well as others.[60] The United States leads the industrialized world in both youth violence and unwanted teen pregnancies, to no small extent because we fail to provide sufficient education, employment, nurturance, and supervision to, especially male, youth. It is proving much more difficult to retrofit masculin-ities than femininities to survive the challenges, opportunities, and hazards of postmodern conditions of work and family life, and our failure to do so carries significant social costs for men, women, children, and social stability. Dada-ism taps into our guilty suppressed, collective awareness of this failure. Instead of addressing it head-on, however, dada-ism resorts to nostalgic fantasies that we can return to a mythic world where Father knew best.

Leaving aside the divisive question of whether the 1950s actually was a time when most men were better and more effective fathers than are most of their offspring today, we cannot return to the economic and cultural conditions that governed gender, family, and work relationships during that era. What we urgently need to do now is to begin to renovate our concepts of fatherhood, parenthood, and "neighborhood" to take account of postmodern conditions. It will take a wide range of creative social initiatives to retool atavistic masculinities effectively. Male breadwinning is no longer an adequate (or widely attainable) definition of effective fathering, but we lack sufficient alternative models of socially desirable forms of masculinity and paternity that are both accessible and attractive to masses of male "displaced breadwinners." On the positive side, increasing numbers of men, disproportionately from middle-class families, are now far more actively involved in nurturant, responsible forms of fathering than ever before—among them the small but rapidly growing percentage of "Mr. Moms" and the broader ranks of fully engaged, egalitarian, coparents in many two-earner families. Moreover, and somewhat paradoxically, time, employment, and money squeezes of postindustrial employment are working to make paternal involvement in child care even more commonplace farther down the income ladder. A 1991 Census Bureau study found that fathers were caring for 20 percent of preschool children while their mothers were at work, a rapid increase in just three years from 15 percent in 1988.[61]

If we wish to promote more of these constructive forms of applied dada-ism, as I, for one, do, then we will have to address some of the sensitive gender and status issues that at-home dads confront. For example, when Tom McKewan made an occupational shift from mechanical engineer to full-time parent to his two preschool daughters, his self-respect suffered: "I lost my self-esteem and respect from peers. I lost adult interaction. I started feeling like a second-class citizen. And I resented everyone."[62] Feminists might readily read McKewan's testimony as further evidence of the second-class status of women's traditional work. While this is certainly true enough, I believe that feminism also bears some secondary responsibility for the low cultural value full-time parenting now "enjoys." Although postindustrial occupational shifts did far more than feminist ideology to erode both the practice and status of full-time domesticity, many early second-wave feminists, including myself, certainly helped to nail the coffin. Critiques of full-time domesticity by White middle-class feminists pervaded the consciousness-raising literature and conversations of the 1960s and 1970s women's liberation movement, including such best-selling classics as Betty Friedan's *The Feminine Mystique* and Marilyn French's *The Women's Room*.[63] More mothers of young children now work outside the home in order to meet their families' economic needs rather than to pursue their personal desires for "self-actualization." Nonetheless, the normalization of paid work for mothers, which feminism helped to legitimate, worked to further disparage the dignity and social status of full-time homemaking. How could we expect men to want to enter a field that even lower-status women have abandoned? Ironically enough, the services of a full-time homemaker-wife have now become so rare (and costly) that the possession of one has begun to make a comeback as a status symbol for affluent career men. It does not augur well for the future success of such families that teenage boys appear more than twice as likely as teenage girls to expect to inhabit them.[64] Feminists might consider taking some initiative to raise social support, status, and economic protection for the minority of men who are willing and able to serve as responsible at-home dads and even for the embattled, defensive ranks of at-home moms.

However, under postindustrial economic conditions, a return to an Ozzie Nelson brand of fatherhood is simply not a viable prospect for most men. A far more promising, not to mention democratic, response to the genuine deficits of parental time and attention that so many "fatherless" children and their caretakers suffer today would be to foster and formalize many more avenues for child-free adults to share some of the joys and burdens of nurturing, supervising, and supporting children. Here I would advocate a range of social inducements and opportunities for adults to enter into multiple paraparenting relationships. We could begin to recognize formally and to facilitate an array of voluntary extended kinship and quasi-parental relationships that already exist on an informal, largely invisible, and therefore more fragile, basis. Building on such models as domestic Big Brother and Big Sister programs, on Latin American comadre and copadre godparent relationships, and on the spontaneous, creative initiatives of numerous exhausted single parents and their caring, and sometimes lonely, child-free associates, legal parents could negotiate agreements with friends, neighbors, and other interested, but legally unrelated, adults to involve the latter in the lives of their children. Such arrangements could be as minimal as "contracting" to serve as backup support to parents for sick care, recreational supervision, holiday companionship, school and hospital visits, and the like; or as major as committing substantial amounts of regular time, money, and labor to help legal parents to bring up their children. We might think of renovating the concept of "foster" parent in this way so that all willing, able, interested, and desirable adults truly might help to foster the parenting of many of our children who suffer from a cultural epidemic of attention deficit disorder that dada-ists mistakenly reduce to fatherlessness.

Efforts to foster diverse patterns of good fathering should constitute a crucial component of a democratic, pluralist politics of and for *families,* rather than The Family. Just as no one family structure is demonstrably best for all, likewise no one type of fathering is desirable or practical. Full-time parenting deserves respect but is unlikely to become a majority practice. What far more men, women, and children desperately need are long-overdue social and occupational reforms to make postindustrial work life compatible with responsible parenting by women and men in a wide array of family patterns. The United States is at the bottom of the industrial pack when it comes to supporting the family needs of its workers. Rather than "fatherlessness" being the "social engine" driving most of our social problems, as Blanken-horn, Popenoe, and their colleagues maintain, the incompatibility of paid work and parenting in the United States is likely the single most crucial source of our "fatherless America."

It is time either to renovate or to warehouse contemporary dada-ism. While politicians and pundits keep competing for an archaic family values crown, equally opportunistic market brands of family values are more current and realistic. On the racks of my local greeting card emporium in May 1996, for example, one could select a "Mother's Day card for Dad" or "a Father's Day card for Mom." These days it is not always easy to decide who is flouting and who is flaunting "conventional aesthetic and cultural values by producing works marked by nonsense, travesty and incongruity." Whereas contemporary dada-ism flaunts its nostalgia for aesthetic and cultural values that are no longer very conventional, it certainly produces too many works marked by intellectual non-sense, a travesty of social science data and logic, and by values increasingly incongruent with the challenging economic and social realities of our contemporary world. Instead of reducing postmod-ern family and social realities to simplistic, repetitive, da-da baby talk, we should be "Bringing Up Father" discourses to a level of maturity, intellectual sophistication, and moral complexity that can assist families to thrive in the twenty-first century.

NOTES

1. *The American Heritage Dictionary of the English Language,* third edition (Boston: Houghton Mifflin, 1992).
2. David Blankenhorn, *Fatherless America: Confronting Our Most Urgent Social Problem* (New York: Basic Books, 1995).
3. Dan Quayle and Diane Medved, *The American Family: Discovering the Values That Make Us Strong* (New York: HarperCollins, 1996), 1.
4. Ibid., 2.
5. Donna Abu-Nasr, "A Romantic Novelty—Dad," *San Francisco Chronicle* October 28, 1996:E5.
6. These articles appear in the *Modern Dad* 2, no.1 (summer 1996).
7. "A Quarterly Newsletter Promoting the Home-Based Father," ParentsPlace.com Home Page, http://www.parentsplace.com.
8. The conference was hosted by the Center for the American Experiment in order to "address the growing problem of children who lack the presence and active involvement of a father in their lives." *Family Affairs* (newsletter) 7, no.1-2 (Spring 1996): 5.
9. The poll, "Fathers in America," was conducted January 11-18, 1996, by the Gallup Organization of Princeton, NJ, for the National Center for Fathering. Results available from NCF.
10. Michael Malone, "Family in Crisis," *Santa Clara Magazine* (Spring 1989), 15.
11. Employing this sort of alarmist rhetoric, New Right forces defeated an effort by California Senator Cranston to pass a day care bill in 1979.
12. See, for example, Rosalind Petchesky, *Abortion and Woman's Choice: The State, Sexuality, and Reproductive Freedom* (Boston: Northeastern University Press, 1984); Carole Joffe, *The Regulation of Sexuality* (Philadelphia: Temple University Press, 1986); and Kristin Luker, *Abortion and the Politics of Motherhood* (Berkeley: University of California Press, 1984).
13. I discuss the turn to pro-family politics among lesbians and gays in chapter 6 of Judith Stacey, *In the Name of the Family: Rethinking Family Values in the Postmodern Age* (Boston: Beacon Press, 1996).
14. PK preacher Tony Evans, as quoted in Joe Conason, Alfred Ross, and Lee Cokorinos, "The Promise Keepers Are Coming: The Third Wave of the Religious Right," *The Nation,* October 7, 1996), 14.
15. *The Jim Lehrer Newshour,"* June 17, 1996.
16. "Achieving Full Fathering: A Conversation on the New Furor over Fathering," panel discussion moderated on-line by Helen Cordes on the Utne Lens, August 1995. http://www.utne.com.
17. Blankenhorn, *Fatherless America,* 117.
18. Ibid.
19. Philip Wylie, *Generation of Vipers,* 20th ed. (New York: Rinehard & Co, 1955; originally published 1942).

20. Ibid., 208.
21. Ibid., 196.
22. Ibid., 208.
23. Ibid., 216.
24. David T. Lykken, "Giving Children a Chance in Life," *Chronicle of Higher Education,* February 9, 1996, B1.
25. Blankenhorn, *Fatherless America,* 1.
26. David Popenoe, "Where's Papa?" *Utne Reader* (September-October 1996), 71.
27. Moynihan as quoted in Hillary Clinton, *It Takes a Village: And Other Lessons Children Teach Us,* (New York: Simon & Schuster, 1996), 40.
28. Daniel Patrick Moynihan, *The Negro Family: The Case for National Action* (Washington, DC: U.S. Department of Labor, 1965).
29. "'Baby Richard' Father Separates From Wife," *San Francisco Chronicle,* January 21, 1997, D1.
30. Blankenhorn, *Fatherless America,* 233.
31. John Leo, "Promoting No-Dad Families," *U.S. News & World Report,* May 15, 1995, 26 .
32. Susan Seligson, "Seeds of Doubt," *Atlantic Monthly* (March 1995): 28.
33. Sec. 3503, "Legislative Accountability," Personal Responsibility Act of 1996, U.S. Congress.
34. See the lengthy, prophetic warning about the tragic consequences of what he accurately defined as the imminent repeal, rather than reform, of welfare which Moynihan inserted into the Congressional Record on December 12, 1995. Reprinted as Daniel Patrick Moynihan, "Congress Builds a Coffin," *New York Review of Books,* January 11, 1996, 33-36.
35. Fund-raising letter for Senator Moynihan mailed in October 1994.
36. Moynihan, "Congress Builds a Coffin," 33.
37. John Gillis, "What's Behind the Debate on Family Values?" Paper delivered at American Sociological Association, Los Angeles, August 6, 1994. For a superb historical treatment of contemporary images of family rituals and values, see Gillis's *A World of Their Own Making: Myth, Ritual, and the Quest for Family Values* (New York: Basic Books, 1996).
38. I discuss the racial political subtext as well as the gender politics of Quayle's attack on Murphy Brown in chapter 3 of *In the Name of the Family.*
39. Kellen's four moms are her birth mother, her birth mother's former lover, a close woman friend of Kellen's birth mother who shared their residence for the first eleven years of Kellen's life, and her birth mother's current committed, live-in partner who has a son conceived through donor insemination. Excerpts of interviews with Kellen and two of her mothers appear in Suzanne Sherman (ed.), *Lesbian and Gay Marriage: Private Commitments, Public Ceremonies* (Philadelphia: Temple University Press, 1992).
40. Gallagher, "The End of Marriage Is Not to Be Celebrated," *The Baltimore Sun,* January 12, 1997, 1F, 4F.

41. Ronald L. Simons et al., *Understanding Differences Between Divorced and Intact Families: Stress, Interaction and Child Outcome* (Thousand Oaks, CA: Sage Publications, 1996), 208.

42. Ibid., 215. Emphasis added.

43. Quoted in "Sociologists Speak to Policy-Makers on Family Issues," *Footnotes* (April 1996): 3.

44. Janet R. Johnston, "Family Transitions and Children's Functioning: The Case of Parental Conflict and Divorce," in Philip A. Cowan et al, (eds), *Family, Self, And Society: Toward a New Agenda for Family Research,* (Hillsdale, NJ: Lawrence Erlbaum Associates, 1993), 197.

45. For a judicious review of the pertinent research, see Frank F. Furstenberg, Jr. and Andrew J. Cherlin, *Divided Families: What Happens to Children When Parents Part* (Cambridge, MA: Harvard University Press, 1991), particularly 70.

46. Simons et al., *Understanding Differences Between Divorced and Intact Families,* 208.

47. Ibid., 210.

48. Gallagher, "The End of Marriage." In this book review of Whitehead's *Divorce Culture* , Gallagher identifies my book, *In the Name of the Family,* as one of three books in 1996 that "suddenly materialized to fight the notion that marriage matters."

49. See, for example, Sanders Korenman, Jane Miller, and John Sjaastad, "Long-Term Poverty and Child Development in the United States: Results from the NLSY" (National Longitudinal Study of Youth), *Children and Youth Services Review* 17 (1995); Greg J. Duncan et al., "Economic Deprivation and Early Childhood Development," *Child Development* 65 (1994); and Timothy J. Biblarz, Adrian Raftery and Alexander Bucur, "Family Structure and Social Mobility," *Social Forces* 75, no.4 (June 1997).

50. Shoshana Alexander, *In Praise of Single Parents: Mothers and Fathers Embracing the Challenge* (Boston: Houghton Mifflin, 1994).

51. Biblarz, et al., "Family Structure and Social Mobility."

52. For the most recent study and a comprehensive review of the research on gay and lesbian parenting to date, see Fiona L. Tasker and Susan Golombok, *Growing Up in a Lesbian Family: Effects on Child Development* (New York: Guilford Press, 1997). I discuss the research on gay and lesbian families in chapter 5 of *In the Name of the Family.*

53. Whitehead, "The Divorce Trap," *New York Times,* January 13, 1997, A15.

54. See Nancy Polikoff, "This Child Does Have Two Mothers: Redefining Parenthood to Meet the Needs of Children in Lesbian-Mother and Other Nontraditional Families," *Georgetown Law Journal* 78 (1990).

55. The girl had lived with her mother since the divorce in 1992, and John Ward filed his custody challenge only after his former wife sought an increase in child support. "Killer Says He's Better for Daughter," *San Francisco Chronicle,* February 3, 1996, A3.

56. Quoted in Elliot Diringer and Robert B. Gunnison, "A Look at Those on Welfare," *San Francisco Chronicle,* February 12, 1997, A17.

57. Quayle, *The American Family,* 2.

58. Piven made this point during a town meeting with Secretary Donna Shalala held during the annual meetings of the American Sociological Association in New York, August 1996. She elaborates it in "Scapegoating the Poor," in Randy Abelda, Nancy Folbre, and the Center for Popular Economics (eds.), *The War on the Poor* (New York: New Press, 1996).

59. "Violence Kills More U.S. Kids," *San Francisco Chronicle,* February 7, 1997, A1, 19.

60. George Gilder, *Men and Marriage* (Gretna, LA: Pelican Publishing Company, 1986).

61. Cited in "At-Home Dad" Press Release/Fact Sheet, http://www.parentsplace.com/At-Home Dad Home Page.

62. Quoted in Julian Guthrie, "Tom, Caroline and Caitlin," *San Francisco Sunday Examiner,* June 16, 1996, A1. This was a Father's Day cover story.

63. Betty Friedan, *The Feminine Mystique* (New York: Norton, 1963); Marilyn French, *The Women's Room* (New York: Summit Books, 1977).

64. In a 1994 poll conducted by the *New York Times* and CBS News, 19 percent of boys claimed they expected their future wives to stay at home, but only 7 percent of the girls expected to stay at home after marriage. Tamar Lewin, "Traditional Family Favored by Boys, Not Girls, Poll Says," *New York Times,* July 11, 1994, A1, C10.

FOUR

GROWING UP WITHOUT A FATHER

Sara McLanahan

IN 1992, when Dan Quayle condemned the television character Murphy Brown for giving birth out of wedlock, he reopened an old debate that quickly became highly polarized. Some people claimed that growing up in a fatherless home was the major cause of child poverty, delinquency, and school failure, while others denied that father absence had any harmful effects. And some objected even to discussing the topic for fear of stigmatizing single mothers and their children.

Not talking about father absence is scarcely an option. More than half of the children born in 1994 will spend some or all of their childhood apart from their biological fathers. If current patterns hold, they will likely experience higher rates of poverty, school failure, and other problems as they grow up. The long-range consequences could have enormous implications.

But what exactly are the consequences—how large? and concentrated among what groups? Do they depend on whether the absence of the father is due to widowhood, divorce, or nonmarital childbirth? Does public support for single mothers inadvertently increase the number of women who get divorced or choose to have a baby on their own?

Many people hold strong opinions about these issues. For example, conservatives such as former Education Secretary William Bennett and Charles Murray believe that single motherhood is so harmful and public support so significant an inducement for unwed women to have babies that it is time to get tough with the mothers. Murray has even proposed denying unwed mothers child support payments from nonresident fathers.[1] In Murray's eyes, mothers are fully responsible for any children they bear "in an age when contraceptives and abortion are freely available." Of the unwed father, Murray says: "As far as I can tell, he has approximately the same causal responsibility as a slice of chocolate cake has in determining whether a woman gains weight."

Meanwhile, some liberal critics see "single mother" as a code word for "Black, welfare mother." They view the focus on out-of-wedlock births and family breakup as an effort to divert public attention and social policy from overcoming racism and lack of opportunity. And then there are the feminists who regard Quayle's attack on Murphy Brown as a symbolic attack on the moral right of women to pursue careers and raise children on their own. So great are the passions aroused by the debate over the morality of single motherhood that a clear-eyed view of the consequences of father absence has been difficult. But to make any progress, we had best know what those are.

DOES FATHER ABSENCE HARM CHILDREN?

Children who grow up apart from their biological fathers are disadvantaged across a broad array of outcomes. As shown in table 4.1, they are twice as likely to drop out of high school, 2.5 times as likely to become teen mothers, and 1.4 times as likely to be idle—out of school *and* out of work—as are children who grow up with both parents.[2]

TABLE 4.1.

THE RISK OF DROPPING OUT OF SCHOOL, IDLENESS, AND TEEN BIRTH, BY FAMILY STRUCTURE

	ALL (%)	TWO-PARENT FAMILY (%)	ONE-PARENT FAMILY (%)
High School Dropout	17	13	29
Idle	13	12	17
Teen Mother	15	11	27

Note: Estimates are adjusted for differences in race, parents' education, number of siblings, and place of residence. Sample is too small to estimate effects for Hispanic children from advantaged backgrounds.

Source: National Longitudinal Survey of Youth, 1979.

Children in one-parent families also have lower grade point averages, lower college aspirations, and poorer attendance records. As adults, they have higher rates of divorce. These patterns persist even after adjusting for differences in race, parents' education, number of siblings, and residential location.

The evidence, however, does not show that father absence is the principal cause of high school failure, poverty, and delinquency. While 17 percent of all children drop out of high school, the dropout rate for children in two-parent families is 13 percent. Thus, the dropout rate would be only 33 percent lower if all families had two parents and if all children currently living with a single parent had the same dropout rates as children living with two parents—a highly improbable assumption. The story is basically the same for the other measures of child well-being. If all children lived with both their biological mothers and fathers, teen motherhood and idleness would be less common, but the bulk of these problems would remain.

The consequences of father absence are not necessarily the same in all kinds of families. Some might suppose that single parenthood would have a larger effect on Black and Hispanic children since, on average, they come from less advantaged backgrounds and their underlying risk of dropping out, becoming a teen mother, and being out of work is greater than that of Whites. Alternatively, others might expect the effect of father absence to be smaller on minority children because single mothers in Black and Hispanic communities are more common, more widely accepted and, therefore, perhaps provided with more support from neighbors and kin.

In our study, we found that, with respect to educational achievement, father absence has the most harmful effects among Hispanics and the least harmful effects among Blacks. Family disruption increases the risk of school failure by 24 percentage points among Hispanics, 17 percentage points among Whites, and 13 percentage points among Blacks. If we look at a different outcome—teenage childbearing—the effects are largest (most harmful) among Blacks, followed by Hispanics and then Whites.

A striking result emerges from the comparison of the percentage increases in risk. Family disruption raises the risk of dropping out of high school by 150 percent for the average White child, by 100 percent for the average Hispanic child, and by 76 percent for the average Black child. Consequently, the dropout rate for the average White child in a one-parent family is substantially higher than the dropout rate of the average Black child in a two-parent family and only two percentage points lower than the dropout rate of the average Black child in a one-parent family. Thus, for the average White child, father absence appears to eliminate much of the advantage associated with being White.

Children from White middle-class families are not immune to the effects of father absence. Consider the children of families in which one parent has at least some college education. If the parents live apart, the probability that their children will drop out of high school rises by 11 percentage points. And for every child who actually drops out of school, there are likely to be three or four more whose performance is affected even though they manage to graduate.

College performance also may suffer. The college graduation rate for White children from advantaged backgrounds is about 9 percentage points lower among children of disrupted families than among children of two-parent families (53 percent versus 62 percent). At the other end of the continuum, children from disadvantaged backgrounds (neither parent graduated from high school) have a bleak future, regardless of whether they live with one or both parents.

ARE CHILDREN BORN OUTSIDE MARRIAGE DOING WORSE?

Some of the current debate presumes that being born to unmarried parents is more harmful than experiencing parents' divorce and that children of divorced parents do better if their mother remarries. Our evidence suggests otherwise (see table 4.2).

Children born to unmarried parents are slightly more likely to drop out of school and become teen mothers than children born to married parents who divorce. But the difference is small compared to the difference between these two groups of children and children who grow up with both parents. What matters for children is not whether their parents are married when they are born but whether their parents live together while the children are growing up.

Children who grow up with widowed mothers, in contrast, fare better than children in other types of father-absent families, especially on measures of educational achievement. Higher income (due in part to more generous social polices toward

TABLE 4.2.

RISK FACTORS FOR CHILDREN IN ONE-PARENT FAMILIES

CONDITIONS OF SINGLE PARENTHOOD	DROPOUT RATE (%)	TEEN BIRTH (%)
Divorce/ separation	31	33
Unmarried	37	37
Widowed	16	21
Stepparent	30	33
Grandmother	60	37
Single father	28	37

Note: Estimates are adjusted for differences in race, parents' education, number of siblings, and place of residence.

Source: National Survey of Families and Households, 1987.

widows), less parental conflict, and other differences might explain this apparent anomaly.

Remarriage is another instance where the conventional wisdom is wrong. Children in stepfamilies do not do better than children whose mothers never remarry. Despite significantly higher family income and the presence of two parents, the average child in a stepparent family has about the same chance of dropping out of high school as the average child in a single-parent family.

Some people believe that single fathers are better able to cope with family responsibilities because they have considerably more income, on average, than single mothers. However, our evidence shows that children in single-father homes do just as poorly as children living with single mothers. Similarly, having a grandmother in the household does not lower the elevated risk of school dropout and teen birth for children in single-mother families.

WHAT ACCOUNTS FOR POOR OUTCOMES?

All of the numbers reported in Tables 4.1 and 4.2 have been adjusted for differences in family background characteristics, such as race, parents' education, family size, and place of residence. Thus, the parents' socioeconomic status cannot explain why children from one-parent families are doing worse.

Unfortunately, we cannot rule out the possibility that the gap stems from some unmeasured difference between one- and two-parent families, such as alcoholism, child abuse, or parental indifference. Only a true experiment could prove that family disruption is really causing children to drop out of school, and no one is willing to assign children randomly to families to answer these questions.

Nevertheless, it is clear that the absence of the biological father reduces children's access to important economic, parental, and community resources. The loss of those resources affects cognitive development and future opportunities. Thus, the evidence strongly suggests that family disruption plays a causal role in lowering children's well-being. When parents live apart, children have less income because the family loses economies of scale and many nonresident fathers fail to pay child support. The average drop in income for White children whose parents separate during the child's adolescence is about $22,000 (in 1992 dollars)—a loss of 40 percent. For Black children, the decline is smaller—about $9,000, a loss of 32 percent. In contrast, when a parent dies, children generally do not experience a major change in their standard of living. Social Security and life insurance help to make up the difference.

Family disruption reduces the time parents spend with children and the control they have over them. When parents live apart, children see their fathers a lot less. About 29 percent do not see them at all. Another 35 percent see them only on a weekly basis. Surprisingly, children born outside of marriage are just as likely to see their fathers on a weekly basis as children of divorced parents. Mothers often find their authority undermined by the separation and consequently have more difficulty controlling their children. One survey asked high school students whether their parents helped them with their schoolwork and supervised their social activities. Students whose parents separated between the sophomore and senior years reported a loss of involvement and supervision compared to students whose parents stayed together.

In addition, family disruption also undermines children's access to community resources or what sociologist James Coleman calls social capital. Divorce and remarriage often precipitate moves out of a community, disrupting children's relationships with peers, teachers, and other adults. During middle childhood and early adolescence, a child in a stable family experiences, on average, 1.4 moves. The average child in a single-parent family is exposed to 2.7 moves; in a stepparent family, the average child experiences 3.4 moves.

Figure 4.1 shows how the loss of economic resources can account for differences between children in one- and two-parent families. The first bar shows the baseline difference between children whose parents divorced during adolescence and children whose parents remained married. The second and third bars show the difference, after adjusting for pre- and postdivorce income (income at age twelve and seventeen). Loss of economic resources accounts for about 50 percent of the disadvantages associated with single parenthood. Too little parental supervision and involvement and greater residential mobility account for most of the rest.

WHY HAS FATHERLESSNESS INCREASED?

Changes in children's living arrangements result from long-standing trends in marriage, divorce, and fertility. Divorce rates in the United States have been going up since the turn of the century and recently

FIGURE 4.1

Income and Divorce

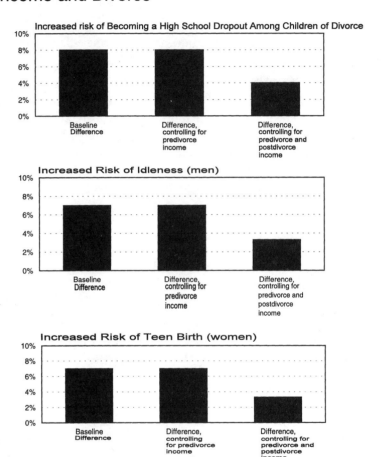

Note: All numbers are adjusted for race, sex, mother's education, father's education, number of siblings and place of residence.

Source: Panel Study of Income Dynamics.

have stabilized at very high levels. Out-of-wedlock birth rates have been going up gradually since at least the early 1940s. After 1960, the age of women at their first marriages began to rise, increasing the proportion of young women who might become unwed mothers. Together, these forces have fueled the growth of single parenthood during the postwar period (see Table 4.3).

These trends exist in all Western, industrialized countries. Divorce rates more than doubled in most countries between 1960 and 1990; in some they increased fourfold. Single parenthood also increased in nearly all the Western countries between 1970 and the late 1980s. Yet the United States has the highest prevalence of single-parent families, and it has experienced the largest increase between 1970 and 1990.

In the view of Murray and other conservatives, welfare benefits in the United States have reduced the costs of single motherhood and discouraged young men and women from marrying. In some parts of the country, welfare may provide poor women with more economic security than marriage does. However, the argument that welfare caused the growth in single-parent families does not withstand scrutiny.

The trend in welfare benefits between 1960 and 1990 does not match the trend in father absence. Welfare and father absence both increased dramatically during the 1960s and early 1970s. After 1974, however, welfare benefits declined, while father absence continued to rise. The real value of the welfare benefit package (cash assistance plus food stamps) for a family of four with no other income fell from $10,133 in 1972 to $8,374 in 1980 and to $7,657 in 1992, a loss of 26 percent between 1972 and 1992 (in 1992 dollars).

Increases in welfare cannot explain why father absence grew among more advantaged women. Since 1960, divorce and nonmarital childbearing have grown among women with a college education, who are not likely to be motivated by the promise of a welfare check.

Table 4.3

International Comparisons: Divorce Rates, Illegitimacy Ratios, and Women's Employment

Country	Divorce Rate[1]		Illegitimacy Ratio[2]		Single Parents[3]	
	1960[4]	1990[5]	1960	1990	1960	1988
United States	9	21	5	28	9	23
Canada	2	12	4	24	9	15
Denmark	6	13	8	46	17	20
France	3	14	6	30	9	12
Germany[6]	4	8	6	11	8	14
Italy	1	2	2	6	NA	NA
Netherlands	2	8	1	11	9	15
Sweden	5	12	11	47	9	13
United Kingdom	2	12	5	28	6	13

NOTES: NA = Not available.

[1] Divorce rate per 1,000 married women.

[2] Percent of all births born to unmarried women.

[3] Percent of all family households that are single-parent. Years 1971 and 1986 for Canada, 1976 and 1988 for Denmark, 1968 and 1988 for France, 1972 and 1988 for Germany, 1961 and 1985 for the Netherlands, 1960 and 1985 for Sweden, 1961 and 1987 for the United Kingdom. Age restrictions for children differ by country.

[4] 1970 for Italy.

[5] 1989 for France; 1988 for United Kingdom.

[6] For former West Germany.

SOURCES: U.S. Bureau of the Census, Statistical Abstract of the United States, 1993; Constance Sorrentino, "The Changing Family in International Perspective," Monthly Labor Review, (March 1990): 41-58.

TABLE 4.4.

INTERNATIONAL COMPARISONS OF PREDICTED POVERTY RATES
OF DIFFERENT TYPES OF FAMILIES: MID-1980S

	POVERTY RATES (%)[1]			
COUNTRY	MARRIED COUPLE FAMILY		SINGLE-MOTHER FAMILY	
	(EMPLOYED MOTHER)	(NONEMPLOYED MOTHER)	(EMPLOYED MOTHER)	(NONEMPLOYED MOTHER)
Netherlands	5.9	3.8	7.2	10.5
Germany	1.0	5.9	13.1	44.4
Sweden	2.3	7.8	3.0	20.3
Canada	5.6	19.1	20.7	62.7
Italy	4.0	16.9	8.9	41.3
United States[2]	9.5	18.7	30.0	69.3
United Kingdom	7.5	17.3	15.0	21.3

NOTES:

[1] Predicted poverty rates controlling for age and education. Poverty is defined as having a total family income less than 50% of the median income for this country (adjusted for family size).

[2] Predicted rates for all races.

SOURCE: Sara McLanahan, Lynne Casper and Annemette Sorensen, "Women's Roles and Women's Status in Eight Industrialized Countries" in *Gender and Family Change in Industrialized Countries* edited by K. Mason and A. Jensen. IUSSP/Oxford University Press, 1995. (Data from the Luxembourg Income Study.)

Welfare payments cannot explain why father absence is more common in the United States than in other industrialized countries. Nearly all the Western European countries have much more generous payments for single mothers than the United States, yet the proportion of children living apart from their fathers is lower in these countries. One way to compare the "costs" of father absence in different countries is to compare the poverty rates of single mothers with those of married mothers (see table 4.4). While single mothers have higher poverty rates than married mothers in all industrialized countries, they are worse off in the United States.[3]

If welfare is not to blame, what is? Three factors seem to be primarily responsible. The first is the growing economic independence of women. Women who can support themselves outside marriage can be picky about when and whom they marry. They can leave bad marriages and they can afford to bear and raise children on their own. Thus, single mothers will be more common in a society where women are more economically independent, *all else being equal.*

American women have moved steadily toward economic independence throughout this century thanks to increased hourly wages, greater control over childbearing, and technological advances that reduce time required for housework.[4] Since the turn of the century, each new generation of young women has entered the labor force in greater proportions and stayed at work longer. By 1970, over half of American women were employed or looking for work; by 1990, nearly three-quarters were doing so. The rise in welfare benefits during the 1950s and 1960s may have made poor women less dependent on men by providing them with an alternative source of economic support. However, welfare was only a small part of a much larger change that was enabling all women, rich and poor alike, to live more easily without a husband.

A second factor in the growth of single motherhood is the decline in men's earning power relative to women's. After World War II and up through the early 1970s, both men and women benefited from a strong economy. While women were becoming more self-sufficient during the 1950s and 1960s, men's wages and employment opportunities were increasing as well. Consequently, while more women could afford to live alone, the economic payoff from marriage continued to rise. After 1970, however, the gender gap in earnings (women's earnings divided by men's earnings) began to narrow. In 1970, female workers earned 59 percent as much as male workers; by 1980, they earned 65 percent as much and by 1990, 74 percent.[5] (These numbers are based on full-time workers between the ages of 25 and 34.) In just two short decades, the economic payoff from marriage had declined by 15 percentage points. Such reductions are likely to increase single motherhood.

The narrowing of the wage gap occurred among adults from all social strata, but the source of the narrowing varied. Among those with a college education, men were doing well, but women were doing even better. Between 1980 and 1990, the earnings of college-educated women grew by 17 percent, while the earnings of college-educated men grew by only 5 percent. (Again, I am referring to full-time workers, aged 25 to 34). Thus, even though the benefits of marriage were declining, women still had much to gain from pooling resources with a man.

The story was much bleaker at the other end of the educational ladder, where between 1970 and 1990, women's earnings stagnated and men's earnings slumped. Between 1980 and 1990, women with a high school degree experienced a 2 percent decline in earnings, while men with similar education experienced a 13 percent decline. This absolute loss in earnings particularly discouraged marriage by some low-skilled men who were no longer able to fulfill their breadwinner role. During the Great Depression, fathers who could not find work sometimes deserted their families as a way of coping with their sense of failure. Again, welfare may have played a part in making single motherhood more attractive than marriage for women with the least skills and education, but only because low-skilled men were having such a hard time and received so little help from government.[6]

The third factor in the growth of single motherhood was a shift in social norms and values during the 1960s that reduced the stigma associated with divorce and nonmarital childbearing. In the 1950s, if a young unmarried woman found herself pregnant, the father was expected to step forward and the couple was expected to marry. By the late 1980s, the revolution in sexual mores permitted young men and women to have intimate relationships and live together outside the bonds of legal marriage.

Attitudes toward individual freedom also changed during the 1960s. The new individualism encouraged people to put personal fulfillment above family responsibility, to expect more from their intimate relationships and marriages, and to leave "bad" marriages if their expectations were not fulfilled. In the early 1960s, over half of all women surveyed agreed that "when there are children in the family, parents should stay together even if they don't get along." By the 1980s, only 20 percent held this view.[7] Once sex and child rearing were "liberated" from marriage and women could support themselves, two of the most important incentives for marriage were gone. When the economic gains from marriage declined in the 1970s, it is not surprising that declines in marriage rates soon followed.

Today, changes in social norms continue to influence the formation of families by making new generations of young adults less trustful of the institution of marriage. Many of the young people who now are having trouble finding and keeping a mate were born during the 1960s, when divorce rates were rising. Many grew up in single-parent families or stepfamilies. Given their own family history, these young people may find it easier to leave a bad relationship and to raise a child alone than to make and keep a long-term commitment.

Compared to the conservative argument that welfare causes single parenthood, these changes provide a more comprehensive and compelling explanation. They explain why single motherhood is more common in the United States than in other industrialized countries: American women are more economically independent than women in most other countries. For this reason alone, father absence should be more common in the United States. In addition, low-skilled men here are worse off relative to women than low-skilled men in other countries. American workers were the first to experience the economic dislocations brought about by deindustri-alization and economic restructuring.[8] Throughout the 1970s, unemployment rates were higher in the United States than in most of Europe, and wage rates fell more sharply here than elsewhere. During the 1980s, unemployment spread to other countries but with less dire consequences for men since unemployment benefits are more generous and coverage is more extensive.

WHAT CAN BE DONE?

Just as father absence has no single cause and no certain outcome, there is no simple solution or "quick fix" for the problems facing children who live apart from their fathers. Strategies for helping these children, therefore, must include those aimed at preventing family breakup and sustaining family resources as well as those aimed at compensating children for the loss of parental time and income.

Preventing Family Breakup and Encouraging Marriage

Parents contemplating divorce need to be informed about the risks to their children if their marriage breaks up. However, it is not clear we can prevent family breakups by making the divorce laws more restrictive, as some analysts suggest. Indeed, more restrictive divorce laws might have the opposite effect. Increasing numbers of young adults are living together and delaying marriage. Making divorce more difficult will only make marriage less attractive relative to cohabitation. A better way to encourage marriage is to make sure that parents—especially poor parents—are not penal-ized when they do get married. Our current system of income transfers and taxation makes marriage a financial liability.[9]

Health care, child care, and housing are three areas in which poor two-parent families receive less government help than well-off two-parent families and impoverished one-parent families. Most middle- and upper-income families receive tax-subsidized health insurance through their employers, and all single-mother families receiving Aid to Families with Dependent Children (AFDC) are eligible for Medicaid. Poor families with a working parent are the least likely to have health insurance. If some variant of the Kennedy-Hatch proposal for universal health care for children up to age eighteen is adopted by Congress, this disincentive to marry will be eliminated.

Similarly, middle- and upper-income families can deduct child care expenses from their income taxes, while single mothers on welfare are eligible for government-subsidized child care. Poor and near poor two-parent families receive virtually nothing in the way of government-subsidized help with child care because they pay no taxes. The same principle applies to housing.

Families that are homeowners—primarily middle- and upper-income households—are allowed to deduct the interest on their mortgage payments from their income tax each year, which amounts to a huge government subsidy. Poor families are eligible for housing subsidies either through vouchers or public housing. Working poor families, in contrast, rarely own their own homes, and if they do, their tax liability is not large enough to allow them to take full advantage of the generous tax deduction that middle-class families receive. Once again, two-parent, near-poor families come out on the bottom in terms of public subsidies.

We now have a very good program, the Earned Income Tax Credit (EITC), for subsidizing the earnings of low-wage workers with children, including married parents. As of 1996, a two-parent family with two children and income below $28,000 received an additional 40 cents for every dollar earned up to a maximum of about $3,400 per year. This program certainly goes a long way toward reducing poverty and economic insecurity in working poor families. Unfortunately, however, the EITC is an earnings subsidy rather than an employment program. Thus, while it can increase the wages of a poor working parent, it cannot help an unemployed parent find a job.

Increasing Economic Security for Single Mothers and Children

Even if we were to remove all the marriage penalties facing poor couples today, some marriages would still break up and some unmarried couples would decide to forgo marriage. In these cases, the government has an obligation to make sure that children's basic needs are covered and that parents contribute their fair share to their child's support. The country now has two major programs that are responsible for protecting "fatherless" children from poverty and economic insecurity: child support enforcement and welfare.

Until recently, we have relied on judicial discretion and parental goodwill to enforce private child support obligations. For children, the consequences have been devastating. Through the law and other means, we must send an unequivocal message to noncustodial fathers (or mothers) that they are expected to share their income with their children, regardless of whether they live with them. This means making sure that all children have a child support award (including children born outside marriage); that awards are adequate and indexed to changes in the nonresident parent's income, and that obligations are paid promptly.

The Family Support Act of 1988 was a giant step toward redressing the failures of our child support system. It required states to increase efforts to establish paternity at birth, to develop standards for setting and updating awards, and to create mechanisms for withholding child support obligations from nonresident parents' earnings. Yet many states have been slow to carry out the Family Support Act. According to recent reports, the gap between what fathers could pay and actually do pay is about $34 billion. The new welfare legislation, the Personal Responsibility and Work Opportunity Act, strengthens child support enforcement in several ways, including streamlining procedures for identifying unwed fathers, automatically withholding child support payments from wages, and requiring states to cooperate with one another in tracking fathers who try to avoid their obligations. These are all excellent policies because they help to prevent poverty in the first place.

Enforcing child support not only increases the income of single mothers but also sends a strong message to men that if they father a child, they become responsible for supporting that child for at least eighteen years. This should make men more careful about engaging in unprotected sex and more reluctant to divorce. My position is diametrically opposed to that of conservatives like Murray who argue that unwed mothers should get no support from the fathers of their children. Instead of getting tough on mothers, we should demand more of fathers. We already have tried tough love on the mothers: we cut welfare benefits by 26 percent between 1970 and 1990, and it didn't work.

Requiring men to bear as much responsibility as women for an "unwanted" pregnancy is not such a radical idea. In fact, it resembles the system that used to prevail in this country before the 1960s, when young men did share the "cost" of an unintended pregnancy: They were expected to marry. The phrase "shotgun marriage" calls to mind a legendary threat the young woman's family might make.

A stricter child support system has its risks. Some people argue that nonresident fathers often are abusive and that forcing these men to pay child support may endanger mothers and children. But most men do not fall into this category. A majority of children should not be deprived of child support because a minority of fathers threaten abuse. Rather, strong steps should be taken to protect single mothers and children (as well as married mothers) from abusive fathers.

Other people object to enforcing child support for fear of overburdening poor fathers. While this problem has long been exaggerated—many fathers can afford to provide much more child support than they now pay—it is true that a substantial proportion of fathers at the bottom tail of the income distribution can pay very little either because they are unemployed or because their wages are so low they can barely cover their own expenses. To help them support their children, nonresident parents—like resident parents—should be guaranteed a minimum-wage job. Those who find a private sector job (or a public nonguaranteed job) should be eligible for the earned income tax credit, even if they are not living with their child.

Making nonresident fathers eligible for the EITC would require restructuring the program. Under the current rules, the benefits go to the household with the dependent child. Under a reformed system, the benefits would go to individuals, and both parents in a two-parent family would be eligible for a subsidy if their earnings were very low. This approach avoids penalizing poor parents who live together.

In addition to enforcing child support obligations, the federal government has a number of programs that provide health care (Medicaid), food and nutrition (Food Stamps; Women, Infants and Children nutrition programs; school lunches), and housing subsidies (Section 8, Public Housing) to poor single mother families. These programs are critical sources of support to single mothers and they should be maintained and expanded as they have been during the past 20 years.

In addition to these in-kind transfers, poor single mothers and children have been *entitled* to a cash benefit—AFDC—until recently. The new welfare reform legislation, the Personal Responsibility and Work Opportunity Act, dramatically changes the rules under which single mothers may receive AFDC. Mothers who receive a benefit will be required to work, after a short period of time, and the amount of time a family can receive a benefit will be limited to a maximum of five years (shorter in some states). In principle, putting more pressure on welfare mothers to enter the labor force may be a good thing. Most married mothers prefer to work outside the home, and most single mothers on welfare probably have the same aspirations. Over the long run, employment should increase a mother's earning power and self-esteem and make her less dependent on government.

The major problem with the work requirements in the new legislation is that neither jobs nor child care are guaranteed. Since working outside the home reduces the amount of time a mother spends with her child, the new legislation could mean less parental involvement and supervision. Whether children are hurt in the long run will depend on how many hours the mother works, whether the children are placed in good day care and after-school programs, and the net income of the family, after deducting for child care and other work expenses. If children have less time with their mothers and their families have no more income, they are likely to be worse off under the new system. If they have less time with their mothers but good child care and more income, they are likely to be better off.

The most serious problem with the new welfare legislation is that it ends the federal *entitlement* to a cash benefit. Under the old system, a poor single mother was entitled to a benefit so long as she passed the "income test." The states put up half the stipend, and the federal government put up the other half. (The federal government paid more than half to mothers in poor states.) Under the new rules, the federal government will give the states a fixed amount. When the money runs out, the states will be on their own. So the next time there is a recession and the welfare roles begin to rise, the states will have to choose between subsidizing 100 percent of the benefit or cutting mothers off. Many analysts fear that some states will choose the latter option.

One step that the federal government might take to help minimize the damage done by the loss of the welfare entitlement is to guarantee a minimum child support payment to all children who live apart from their fathers. A benefit worth up to $2,000 per year for one child would be paid either by the father or by the government.[10] The benefit should be conditional on having a court-ordered child support award, so that single mothers have an incentive to obtain an award, and it should be implemented in conjunction with automatic wage withholding so that fathers cannot shirk their responsibility. As yet, no state in the United States has tried such a program, even though the bipartisan National Commission on Children, headed by Senator Jay Rockefeller in 1991, recommended that demonstrations be conducted and even though similar programs exist in several other countries (France, Sweden).[11] In the current political environment, the public would more likely support a guaranteed child support benefit that was linked to fathers paying their fair share than a cash transfer that was not conditional on fathers' involvement.

Local governments and community organizations also should do more to help children in fatherless families. They could extend the school day or use school facilities to house extracurricular activities that would offset the loss of parental time and supervision. Mentoring programs also could be used to connect children to adults in their community. In April of 1997, the president held a "summit" in Philadelphia that was headed up by General Colin Powell and attended by former Presidents Ford, Carter, and Bush. The summit was designed to encourage volunteerism and build new community partnerships between business, local government, and nonprofit organizations. One of the stated goals of the summit is to increase mentoring programs for youth and provide more "safe places" for youth during after-school hours. Whether communities and local governments will be able to follow through on this initiative remains to be seen. But children with nonresident fathers are likely to benefit disproportionately from such programs.

The recommendations just listed are driven by three underlying principles. The first is that something must be done immediately to reduce the economic insecurity of children in father-absent families. Low income is the single most important factor in accounting for the lower achievement of these children, and, therefore, raising income should be a major priority. The federal government has demonstrated considerable success in reducing the economic insecurity of the elderly. There is no reason why we cannot do the same for children.

A second principle is shared responsibility. The costs of raising children must be distributed more equally between men and women and between parents and nonparents. At present, mothers bear a disproportionate share of the costs of raising children. Fairness demands that fathers and society at large assume more responsibility.

Third, and most important, programs for child care, health care, and income security should be universal—available to all children and all parents. The problems facing single parents are not very different from the problems facing all parents. They are just more obvious and more pressing. Universal programs avoid the dilemma of how to help children in one-parent families without creating economic incentives in favor of one-parent families. Universal programs also reinforce the idea that fatherlessness is a risk shared by a majority of the population. Growing up without a father is not something that happens to other people and other people's children. It can happen to us and to our children's children.

NOTES

This chapter draws heavily on the research reported in the author's book *Growing up With a Single Parent* and is adapted from an article that appeared in the *American Prospect* in the summer of 1994 ("The Consequences of Single Parenthood" Summer 48-58.)

The research was supported by grants from NICHD HD29601, HD19375, Office of Population Research, Princeton University Center Grant 5P30HD/AG32030, and the Lowenstein Foundation. I would like to thank Melanie Adams for editorial and technical assistance.

1. Charles Murray, "Keep It in the Family." *London Sunday Times,* op-ed piece, November 14, 1993.
2. Sara McLanahan and Gary Sandefur, *Growing Up With a Single Parent* (Cambridge: Harvard University Press, 1994).
3. Sara McLanahan, Lynne Casper, and Annemette Sorensen, "Women's Roles and Women's Poverty" in *Gender and Family Change in Industrialized Countries,* K. Mason and A. Jensen (eds.) (Oxford: Clarendon Press, 1995), 258-278.
4. Barbara Bergman, *The Economic Emergence of Women* (New York: Basic Books, 1986).
5. Daphne Spain and Suzanne Bianchi, *Balancing Act* (New York: Russell Sage, 1996).
6. William Julius Wilson, *When Work Disappears* (New York: Knopf Publishers, 1996).
7. Arland Thornton and Donald Camburn, "The Influence of the Family on Premarital Sexual Attitudes." *Demography* 24(3), 323-340.
8. Wilson, 1996.
9. Irwin Garfinkel, "Economic Security for Children: From Means Testing and Bifurcation to Universality." in *Social Policies for Children,* I. Garfinkel, J. Hochschild, and S. McLanahan (eds.) (Washington D.C.: The Brookings Institute, 1996).
10. Irwin Garfinkel, *Assuring Child Support* (New York: Russell Sage, 1993).
11. National Commission on Children, *Beyond Rhetoric: A New American Agenda for Children and Families* (Washington D. C.: United States Government Printing Office, 1991).

FIVE

"THIS RIVER RUNS DEEP":
FATHER MYTHS AND SINGLE MOTHERS IN POOR AMERICA

Lisa Dodson

> My mother would say, ". . .you have to hold onto family, cause
> that's really all you got that matters" . . . and I realized that she
> was what kept us going, kept us being a family. Now I say to
> my kids, 'Look, I know it gets hard but we'll get by cause your
> ma's not letting this family down.' I tell them 'I am like a river
> that keeps on rolling and this river runs deep.'"
>
> —From a life-history interview with Renata,
> age thirty-two, raising two children alone, 1993.

THERE IS LITTLE DOUBT THAT IN LOW-INCOME AMERICA, single-mother families endure an exaggerated degree of economic hardship and social troubles.[1] Furthermore, this is the fastest growing segment of people who are poor in this nation.[2] Without the resources available to nonpoor families, many single-mother families have difficulty obtaining basic needs, staying safe, living in secure housing, offering children decent education, and gaining access to opportunities needed by all people to develop fully.[3] In a land which, in this decade alone, boasts of a plethora of new millionaires,[4] America also has the highest rate of child poverty of industrialized nations,[5] and many of these children reside in single-mother families. Yet while many people deplore the suffering of children, reducing public aid to poor families is common policy practice these days.[6] In America, the growing convention is that family security is only for those who can afford to buy it. In the absence of any national commitment to children and family life, all those "other" families raising children in low-income America are without access to basic security and safety. Reflecting this social ethic of the times, most policy proposals are bent on modifying the people within families[7] and not on investing in them or altering the economic and social forces which surround them.

Running throughout much of the recent discourse about the problems associated with mother-only families is a sharp focus on the impressive absence of fathers and paternal resources. While there is no national consensus on all the effects of father absence, there is abundant evidence that the father's return could significantly enhance the economic well-being of families. Fathers also may increase parenting resources and perhaps offer children the valuable experience of an involved man in their lives, supporting socialization and future aspirations.[8] Some social critics, leaders of religious movements, and policy analysts postulate that the father's return would reclaim a family life that is not only better for family members but better for society at large.[9] The particularly attractive picture of father coming home satisfies both material needs and intangible longings and, one might note, requires no public investment.

There are flaws to this premise, not the least of which being that many low-income men do not abandon the role of partner or parent casually, but in the context of profound economic and social pressures that stymie their ability to contribute what they believe they should.[10] Many other men, judged as absent because they do not provide economic support, may in fact be largely present and involved but reduced to nonentity status by a policy yardstick which measures little beyond monetary support.[11] And, too, it is worth noting that some families are far better off without men who are abusive and conflict-ridden, whether they have wealth that they share or not. Yet I would sound a strong cautionary note about an ideological enthusiasm for the return of fathers as the solution to the troubles experienced by low-income, mother-only families. Whether castigating poor men (particularly men of color) or examining the psychology of other men (particularly men with money), the focus on father as savior may serve to deepen popular misconceptions about the millions of single mothers who struggle to raise their children.

It is true that both low-income women and men are reproved for out-of-wedlock fertility, with particularly venal attention paid to African American non-marital births. Yet women are far more likely to be there to attend to the subsequent eighteen years of raising children, doing so under harsh public inspection. Public assistance systems are ever-present to document the ongoing and grinding effects of family poverty for all the world to see. Yet we have no public record of the gargantuan effort and litany of achievements which are the norm in mother-only families. Against a backdrop of pejorative images in the media, up against the rhetoric of political leaders deriding poor mothers, a father renaissance could affirm the important role of low-income fathers at the cost of deepening a distortion about single mothers in poor America.

In this chapter I use three excerpts from fifty life-history interviews (analyzed in subsequent focus groups) with diverse, low-income single mothers to identify strengths and achievements largely ignored in this and other discourses on family policy. In the course of this research, it was found that most women affirm the importance of men in children's lives, and in fact long for them and would welcome their positive involvement. But they echo each other across race, ethnic, and family differences, and their challenge is fairly simple. If we as a nation of people hold children and family dear, some serious work must be done to offset the relentless hardships that women face as they raise the future mothers and fathers of low-income America. And while we set about gaining an understanding of father absence and perhaps even succeed in coaxing some men home, we might learn the truth about those who raise the families in the here and now.

As a poor-all-her-life Italian woman of seventy told her grand-daughter, who (in 1994) was raising her twin toddlers on her own, "Don't get stuck in bitter words. The man, he struggles and the woman, she struggles, . . . don't take one against the other . . . that's just a waste of time. . . . It is stupid thinking. You have to do what's right for the babies and act big." Listening to her formulate this blunt view of social ethics, a diverse group of women nodded as one.

"TYPICAL WELFARE MOTHERS"

Of the fifty women (ages twenty-four to forty-eightish) whom I interviewed, more than half were originally teen mothers, half came from single-mother families (often with other adults involved), and most had received income-based public assistance at some point while growing up. Half had interrupted secondary school education, yet all but three had returned to get a high school diploma at some point in their lives. Ten women had been married, with three of the fifty receiving formal child support. (Many women received informal support from the fathers of their children and some from their "in-law" families, as well.) All had relied on Aid for Families with Dependent Children (AFDC) at some period, with a range of just less than one year to over twelve years, the majority needing welfare for four to five years. Eight women had been homeless for a time while raising a family, and most reported frequent moves while their children were young.

Taken as a group, these single mothers' experiences were similar to those of many women on welfare during the late 1980s and the early 1990s. More pointedly, they easily could be regarded as "typical welfare mothers" and some women used that terminology themselves, but not without irony.

Speaking Our Minds

Bernadette. In 1993, Bernadette was a twenty-eight year-old Irish woman whose parents were born in Ireland, "off the boat. . . . well, actually off a plane but the way they looked it could have been a refugee boat." She herself identified with that faraway island despite the fact that she had never been there. Bernadette had her first child at the age of eighteen, leaving high school early in her senior year, but she reflected, "I was already a year left back and wasn't getting anywhere with school." Bernadette had married her boyfriend of four years ("We met in the eighth grade") and had moved in with him, but he left before her son was two years old. She then had moved to a low-income neighborhood in Boston, alternating between work and welfare as layoffs, lack of affordable child care, and her fragile job skills led her fumbling along in Boston's labor market. When she met her second boyfriend, Bernadette had thought the hardest times were over. "He was steady, he loved my son, it was perfect." While she and her second partner, both divorced, had chosen not to marry right away, they had two daughters in three years. Then the meat packing plant where her "husband" had worked for eight years shut down, and everything seemed to change. Bernadette recalled how withdrawn and angry he had become, and then he had begun to drink.

Bernadette had moved out with her children and moved again and again, a total of six times in ten years. She recalled this decade as "gypsy years," as settling in and trying to juggle and then having things fall apart. She recalled how the first several years of her children's lives had been marked by family violence, months of isolation and loneliness, and the contempt of people who "think they're better than you are and they make your kids feel small. . . ."

And she recounted constant exhaustion as having been an overwhelming force in her life. "I was so tired that for years, I would fall asleep as soon as I sat down on the T (subway). The rock, rock, rocking would put me and my three kids out like a light. We would miss our stop sometimes, sometimes the kids would be late for school. . . ."

Yet Bernadette had also become determined to finish her high school education. For a long time that goal and keeping her children safe had been all she hoped to accomplish. Then, in 1993, with her diploma and a part-time job, Bernadette was looking for a baby-sitter to watch her children in the afternoon so that she could attend classes at a community college. But she had no luck; she could offer so little pay and she was choosy about who should be with her children, "'specially my girls, you know, you can't be too careful 'bout that, you hear a lot about these mothers leaving their kids with someone and some creep gets at them."

When I asked Bernadette what kinds of policies or programs would have helped her, could help other young women in her place, she answered immediately. Above anything else, a woman and children need to be safe, need some security.

Look, my kids moved and moved because we could not find a safe place to live that we could afford. And don't start telling me about this HUD program and that 'cause I have heard it all. My kids had only two years starting and finishing the same class in the same school 'cause either the building got shut down [where she lived], we got evicted 'cause I couldn't keep up, or the place was so dangerous I just up and yanked them out and we moved to another apartment. They fell back in school and that just made them feel worse. We need to have homes for people raising children where they are safe. I'm not saying luxury condos, okay? Just safe and, like your kid knows he's going to be there for a time, like it's a home. I don't care if there's a man or no man in the house, kids need to know they have some kind of home or they can't pay attention, and then everybody comes saying they got attention problems and this and that. Yeah, you bet my kids got attention problems 'cause they don't know what's going to be there. . . . Except me . . . they know I'm going to be there, you know, come hell or high water . . . Ma's there.

Bernadette laughed as she remembered a recent conversation with her children. Later she explained, "Well, I'm not always the sweet little mother. I'm kind of in-your-face mother, but I think that's where they want me. So they don't ever think I'm slipping away . . . something has got to be right there and that something is me."

Bernadette shared the outlook of many other women whom I have interviewed over the years. She was quick to speak her mind and quite critical about her own moments of despair when her children needed her to be brave and confident. And she was deeply sensitive to the scorn that she believed is reserved for women who need public assistance. But above all, she was angry about what she regarded as a class-based disinterest in her children's development. Looking me in the eye, Bernadette asked, "Look, even if I am blamed 'cause I could make it, and couldn't keep my man straight or what all they say . . . is that my kids' fault? How are they supposed to do better . . . just you tell me that." Bernadette was convinced her children were not valued or treated with respect, and she had a big bone to pick with people who "turn their backs" on low-income families. While many of the African American mothers with whom I spoke regarded this treatment as a product of racism and many of the Latinas saw it as American prejudice against Spanish-speaking people, their words seemed to spring from the same tenacious place, a common woman's knowledge of society's attitude toward her children.

Annette. Annette was also twenty-eight in 1992, when I met with her several times over the course of a month. She was proudly Puerto Rican and often would point to her ethnic heritage as the context for some key issues in her life. "You can say what you like,

Hispanic women are going to have childrens even if that man isn't going to stay. It is part of our values, being a good mother, taking care of the family, being home and keeping them safe." This was the life which Annette's mother had taught her daughters in New York City, growing up with an extended family crammed into a two-bedroom apartment in the Bronx. "We spent a lot of time out on the front steps, with the music on and peoples dancing and kids yelling. My cousins and me were like sisters and brothers. I wanted to have children from the time I was a baby myself."

Annette and her older sister had watched the family grow larger and then break up as their uncle left their aunt and their father had become overwhelmed by two women and five children to feed. She believed that quietly, her parents looked forward to the girls reaching the age of sixteen, "which for them was the age of becoming a woman, coming out to the world which means meeting a husband and moving out." But Annette's sister left home before her sixteenth birthday, running away with a man of twenty-five, who, as it turned out, was already married. Annette believed that this event, which had so shocked the whole clan, had been destined to occur, that her sister made it evident that she was going to run. "They tried to keep us home all the time, watching the babies, cleaning and cooking and all that. Boys can go out into the street, but we had to stay home, couldn't even stay after school to be in the play or anything like that."

I asked Annette if she thought this was only the way of Latino families, if it wasn't the case that other cultures also tend to keep girls close to home and busy with house chores. She asserted, yes, it is common, but for Puerto Rican families, it is particularly the practice. "My father thought every man was out to molest his daughters, he was always talking about them that way. And then my sister goes off and so it sort of proved his point."

Annette left home in the prescribed way, married at the age of seventeen to a twenty-one-year-old son of a local minister who moved them up to Boston. Her family had been proud of her, delighted with the birth of her son and aghast when she told them she and her husband had separated. "We were too young, he was such a child really. His mother had spoiled him and he wanted me to do the same. It was one thing before I had a child of my own but after . . . come on." Annette's husband, clearly unprepared for the demands of father-hood, had thought that his contribution was bringing home a paycheck. The fact that Annette was trying to take a data-entry class one evening each week and had to work as well was a source of great conflict. Eventually Annette had to drop out of the course, which hurt her prospects at her job. "They [her employer] couldn't get it, you know, they had put out the money for me to do the course and here's this Spanish girl, can't even make her classes. Well, if my baby is all alone, no, I can't make my class, end of story."

After Annette had separated from her husband, she moved in with her aunt, who also had moved to Boston. She was very glad to have someone to go to, particularly because her parents believed that she should come home immediately, "but what with my sister back home with her babies and all that . . . I knew my chance was here." During the next few years, Annette had often been alone, depressed, and filled with a sense of failure. She had been employed at times, on welfare at times, and trying hard to keep up her son's spirits. After having attempted a reconciliation with her husband for a year, she gave birth to a daughter. But after that, they were divorced. She mused over the evolution of her relationship with her former husband, who has remarried and has two more children. "I was a girl when we met and married and the baby and then I started to be a woman. After I had to go it alone for a while, I just couldn't be that girl . . . she was gone. You can't do like I had to do, to get through all that pain and your baby sad and having problems and what not. . . . I mean, that girl was gone, I'm sorry if he didn't like the woman, but that girl was gone. I put her away."

In 1992, Annette was employed on a full-time basis in com-puter services for an insurance company, still living with her aunt. Her children are both doing well, but her son has an "anxiety thing

. . . they got a name for it. When I leave him he gets really nervous, he used to breathe too hard and even throw up. He is better now, but sometimes like when school starts he gets back into that, I got to talk really quiet to him and make him remember, we been through much worse and we got through. I wish the teachers had more patience with him, he needs patience, you know?"

It seemed to me that after a tough ten years, Annette's life was much improved. I asked her how she felt about how things had worked out for her. She was thoughtful about her place in the world. Tracing that long decade in the interviews had made her reflective and also made her proud. But it was hard to reconcile this life with the one she had anticipated as a girl. "We [Latinas] expect to have this family, you know. I mean, everyone's got problems but I never thought I would be here with children and no man. And you know what? I have this nice boyfriend now, kind, nice, flowers, you know what I am saying? And me, I'm not about marrying him. . . . He doesn't really get it but I just don't think so. I seen my sister be beaten down, you know, and me I was so depressed about it all. Mens have got their troubles, I know, but I got to go on and do what I got to do."

Annette captured a theme which many women shared, particularly older women as they looked back over their own lives. Early images of their role in the world were steeped in cultural and gender images, diverse in some ways, similar in others. Many women believe that, as girls, they absorbed the message that they should focus on family, domestic responsibilities, and seek out male partners as affirmation of their gender and a coming-of-age. Without alternatives, this often led to early attachment to male partners, relationships that were immature and unstable. Left with babies and a world which offered no quarter, these young women would reach down inside and find a strength which brought them through hard times, abuse, isolation, and social stigma. Finding these inner resources was essential, they told me, but it meant leaving something else behind. Annette referred to what was abandoned as "that girl." Another woman, more contemptuous, called it "staying dumb." And still another mused, "that big-eyed doll-baby thing that men likes in a girl. Well, pardon me, she gone."

She does not survive in the world these women know.

Emma. Emma spoke of another kind of strength, the power of a moral covenant, which she believed was a source of many women's survival. Emma shared the view of many people who face ongoing economic trouble, that what happens to the people around you is part of your life.

Emma, an African American woman, was thirty-four when I met with her over the summer of 1993. Emma described being a little girl and how, during her annual summer visits, she would accompany her grandmother as she delivered food to some families in a distant Alabama community. This small, voluble woman would lecture Emma and explain to her the duties of family and of being good neighbors. "You don't make a fuss of it, remember," Emma reported her grandmother had told her. "You go by, you talk and ask how things are doing, how's the baby feeling. You let her have a chance to talk, maybe cry. Then you just pass over the basket, like 'oh, by the way . . . here's this.' You move on quick then so's she doesn't feel shamed by it."

As Emma grew into adolescence, she recalled how quaint this tiny woman had been, how "country" and old-fashioned. Yet when she grew into womanhood, it became clear to Emma that this little woman was deep in her bones.

"Black folks have always had to help each other out 'cause for so long, no one else cared whether we got by, whether our children survived." Emma was careful to reassure me, lest I "take her wrong," that she did not believe all White people were incapable of compassion. As did many women, White women and women of color, Emma repeated the open-minded refrain, that there are some good and some bad of all peoples. In fact, she believed that her grandmother's practice of sharing what little you have is universal, undertaken by different people, country people and city people, Hispanic people and Whites and "Black folks." But at heart it is a similar code born from common women's knowledge of this life. To Emma, this was a contract to which all people should subscribe, the notion that you have obligations beyond "just taking care of your own."

Emma's own life has been a hard one. She had her first child young but managed to complete high school, missing only two weeks of classes. She attended her graduation with family and friends and a four-month-old daughter. Emma's boyfriend had been very proud of his daughter, and they had worked hard not to "bust up just as soon as the baby is born" as so many other adolescent relationships seemed to do. But living in her "mother-in-law's" apartment had been cramped and tense for both Emma and her boyfriend, Earl. "I knew she didn't want me there but she was a Christian woman and thought she had to help us out. But she would always take Earl's side with everything, like say he shouldn't have to take the baby and all. I was with people who didn't want me, only my daughter." Emma moved back to her parents' house despite her father's anger at her having a baby out-of-wedlock. She slept on a sofa with her baby in a playpen beside her and would "cry all night long."

Emma explained that her parents were religious people and were ashamed of her, thought that she had brought them down in the eyes of their neighbors and church-going friends. On the other hand, they loved little Adrienne and they did not want Emma to live with people who did not care for her. It became clear to Emma that, while Earl was still very attached to his daughter and would regularly take her for visits, he had moved on in his life.

Over the next two years, Emma juggled raising her daughter, attending courses to become a practical nurse, and working part-time at a hospital. When her parents moved back to their birthplace in the South, Emma moved in with her boyfriend of almost two years, which turned out to be "the biggest mistake of my life." She had a son, Damien, at the age of twenty-three and was homeless by the age of twenty-four.

Ten years later, she had an apartment near the hospital where she worked as a pediatric nurse, her daughter was an honors student in a prestigious Boston high school, and her son was doing well in Catholic middle school. Emma took her children to work at a soup kitchen one night each week, and she coordinated a summer camp program through her church, "to get city kids out of the streets for a couple of weeks and give some tired moms a chance to think."

When I asked Emma what made it possible for her to go from living in a woman's shelter to where she is now, a respected health professional, she spoke a lot about faith. Emma described hers as a religious faith, but also a faith in people and above all in herself. And she told me, laughing, that Earl turned out to be a dear friend, after two years of mutual recriminations. Not only has he stayed in touch with Adrienne, attending school functions and bragging about her intelligence ("He says she's going to be the first college graduate in his family and I say 'Yeah, and the first Black woman neurosurgeon in America'"), but he also took to Damien right from the start. He asked Damien to join him when he brought Adrienne over to visit her grandparents and he even showed up at the boy's basketball games, shouting with the best of them. "He hasn't got a son, he had two more daughters but no son. And you know one day when he visited us and I was feeling blue as the ocean with my babies and all, he told me 'give them to me for the day.' When he brought them back he had bought Addy new shoes and a coat and that, and he had bought the same for my son. From that day on, he always showed my son love."

In fact, Emma and Earl have helped each other out, trading childcare for all four of their children and ". . . being around to talk sometimes. Earl's really a good man, not strong enough for the way things got in our lives, but men can't handle some things."

I asked Emma about that, the idea that men are not able to face certain realities, and she pondered the idea. She told me, "I don't know about your men, but you see, our men have the wind at their back . . . they have so much to face and no place that's theirs . . . that's about them. So they turn their back." It seemed such a clear picture as Emma quietly described it, for all her own pain and anger at Earl. And it turned out to be a picture that many women could grasp, listening to her story in focus-group discussions. Most women would nod their heads at the complexity of the conditions which Emma and Earl faced, conditions in which some people stumble around yet try to hold onto their connection. Emma found she could accept the kindness and help which Earl could afford and so he had become a welcome support.

In a later interview she told me, "I am raising Damien to believe he will have to do just like the girl does, none of this 'well, I'm the man' trash. He does dishes and he does cleaning, we get the mops out and that mop don't say 'girls only' on it, now does it? But I run scared with him, especially now, as he gets close to being a teen, more scared than ever I was for Addy."

TALKING IT OVER

Wrapped around much of the discourse about family life is a largely shared conviction about the identity of women who head so many poor American families. Often referred to as irresponsible, non-working, and dysfunctional, this picture has enjoyed precious little public challenge. And certainly there are people in low-income communities (and in upper-income communities, for that matter) who cannot rise up to family pressure, to troubled children, and to juggling all the demands of hard-pressed family life.

Yet I have long been impressed by the contrast between so many of the women I have met over the years and the common image of single mothers who raise poor children. It is a great fracture that thrives in this nation. And so I took the data back again and again, and pursued this rift with groups of low-income women who wanted to "talk it over."

Eleanor, in her fifties and White, explained it simply in one focus group. She said that blame is a psychological response to problems that seem too complex. "You got to have someone to blame, or it don't feel right. Now who you going to blame, sure the man, but he's mostly gone. And the kids, well, they wait till their teens and then get to blaming them. But meanwhile, there's that mom, all shabby and needs the apartment voucher, the food stamps, the welfare check, and she's down in the mouth anyway. She's perfect to blame, right?"

A young Haitian woman, Crystal, agreed with this, but believed race was a big factor. "They [White, middle-class people] think we don't really have the same ways as they do. They don't know us, how hard we work, all the pain we come [referring specifically to Haiti]. That's why they shut us out, you know, not like Russians and Polish people, they shuts us out. But they don't really know about us."

Carole, an African American woman in her late twenties, thought race was part of it, but also that it was the product of American social attitudes. "They teach these kids to be about me, me, me. The White kids have their cars and their own phone lines and the new clothes. . . . [in response to some objections from other women she modified this]. Okay, Okay, not all, but like out in [suburban towns]. So they're like, hey, we got this and that and why should we bother with you? My child went to Metco [a program which buses children out of the city to suburban schools] and like, he's over here with his friends and they're over there. We teach our kids it's more than just me . . . but that's not the way they see it."

Carole's comment provoked some conflict. Another older African American woman, Ester, shook her head and said, "Look at our children out there and tell me they're any different. They be about 'get my sneakers' and 'my colors' and all that. I mean, some of our kids are hardworking and some mothers and fathers try to do all they can here in the city and out there is 'La-La Land' [a reference which delighted the group], but it's not one or the other. I think that's ignorant."

But why is it, I asked, that women, who raise children and need help, get portrayed as nonworkers and dysfunctional?

Oh well, *that*, they said, and seemed this time in full accord. Ester spoke for the group. "Who all writes those newspapers, then? Who all wrote the history books? When did any rich man take care of babies with no money, no help, no place that's a home?" Crystal interrupted her to insert "And no respect neither. . . ." Ester continued, "I'm not saying all these girls are good mothers and all, 'cause some of them I'd like to take out back myself. But most work their tails off to just get by."

Eleanor joined in. "There is nothing harder than that. I been on welfare, I been off, back on, been a single mother and a single grandmother. I held a job. I held two jobs. You want to talk about work, raise babies with no money. . . . out there . . . makes me mad, I'm gonna say something impolite."

Go ahead on, the others told her.

And getting fathers to stay home? That would be nice, many women thought, as long as he was healthy and committed. It is good to have a man there as part of the family. Good for the kids. But in the meantime, there are children to raise and business to take care of, so most single mothers do the job "best as they can."

"ACTING BIG"

The call for a return of fathers to low-income, single-mother families feels good to many and has the virtue of being tax-free. Yet this solution suggests the problem of poor families is simply the people who form them, irresponsible fathers who leave and dysfunctional mothers who don't. It leaves unchallenged the growing popularity of policies that promote an American family apartheid, increased tax relief and capital gains for some families, the loss of housing and food for others. Father-as-savior also avoids the essential structural challenge—the need to change those structures that give rise to this increasingly stratified family life in America.

As numerous single mothers have indicated, they share the quest for husband/father as they face the conditions of life outside the shelter of middle-income America. Yet many would point out that as men grapple with the ways this society affects them and social critics chide them to go home, there are women at work, holding fast, "acting big."

NOTES

1. Valerie Polakow, *Lives on the Edge: Single Mothers and Their Children in the Other America* (Chicago: University of Chicago Press, 1993); Sara McLanahan and Karen Booth, "Mother Only Families: Problems, Prospects, and Politics," *Journal of Marriage and the Family* 51 (1989): 557-580; Irwin Garfinkel and Sara S. McLanahan, *Single Mothers and Their Children: A New American Dilemma* (Washington DC: Urban Institute Press, 1986); Sheila B. Camerman and Alfred J. Kahn, *Mothers Alone: Strategies for a Time of Change* (Dover, CN: Auburn House Publishing Company, 1988).

2. Donald Hernandez, *America's Children: Resources from Family, Government, and the Economy* (New York: Russell Sage Foundation, 1993).

3. Kathryn Edin and Laura Lein, *Making Ends Meet: How Single Mothers Survive Welfare and Low-Wage Work* (New York: Russell Sage Foundation, 1997); Ruth Sidel, *Keeping Women and Children Last: America's War on the Poor* (New York: Penguin Books, 1996); Elizabeth A. Mulroy, *Women as Single Parents: Confronting Institutional Barriers in the Courts, the Workplace, and the Housing Market* (Dover, CN: Auburn House Publishing Company, 1988).

4. "Too Rich?: The well-to-do are getting rich faster than ever before. Their problem: How to spend it all," *Boston Globe,* July 27, 1997, E1.

5. Rebecca M. Blank, *It Takes a Nation: A New Agenda for Fighting Poverty* (New York: Russell Sage Foundation, 1997); Hernandez, *America's Children.*

6. Christopher Jencks and Kathryn Edin, "Do Poor Women Have the Right to Bear Children?" The *American Prospect* 20 (1995): 43-52; Mimi Abramovitz, *Regulating the Lives of Women: Social Welfare Policy from Colonial Times to the Present* (Boston: South End Press, 1988); Michael B. Katz, *In the Shadow of*

the Poorhouse: A Social History of Welfare in America (New York: Basic Books, 1986).

7. L. W. Hoffman, "Increasing Fathering: Effects on Mother," in Lamb and Sagi (eds.), *Fatherhood and Family Policy* (Hillsdale, NJ: Lawrence Erlbaum, 1983); N. Radin, "Primary Caregiving and Role-Sharing Fathers," in Michael E. Lamb, (ed.), *Nontraditional Families: Parenting and Child Development* (Hillsdale, NJ: Lawrence Erlbaum, 1982); Frank Furstenberg "Good Dads-Bad Dads: Two Faces of Fatherhood," in Andrew Cherlin (ed.), *The Changing American Family and Public Policy* (Washington: The Urban Insitute Press, 1988).

8. David Blankenhorn, *Fatherless America: Confronting Our Most Urgent Social Problem* (New York: Basic Books, 1995).

9. R. D. Parke and B. Neville, "Teenage Fatherhood," in Hofferth and Hayes (eds.), *Risking the Future: Adolescent Sexuality, Pregnancy and Childbearing* (Washington D.C.: National Academy Press, 1987); Frank F. Furstenberg, "Fathering in the Inner City: Paternal Participation and Public Policy," in William Marsiglio (ed.), *Fatherhood: Contemporary Theory, Research and Social Policy* (Beverly Hills, CA: Sage Publications, 1995).

10. Mercer L. Sullivan, "Absent Fathers in the Inner City," in William Julius Wilson (ed.), *The Ghetto Underclass* (Newbury Park, CA: Sage Publications, 1989).

11. Katherine Newman, "Working Poor, Working Hard: Plight of the Working Poor," *The Nation* 263 (1996): 20-23; Edin and Lein, *Making Ends Meet;* Sidel, *Keeping Women and Children Last;* Abramovitz, *Regulating the Lives of Women.*

Six

The Lost Children

Jean Bethke Elshtain

WE ARE A SOCIETY THAT PRIDES ITSELF on its collective move from a world in which judgments of the behavior of others came too easily to one in which we are invited not to judge at all. But judgment—as discernment, a process of sifting relevant factors, sorting out the important from the less important—is the heart of political life. Politics has never, save in its most vulgar and often dangerous manifestations, been a process of making normative whatever the current social trends happen to be. Yet that is precisely what is going on at present in the debates about teen pregnancy and the phenomenon of fatherlessness. In their rush to defend single teen mothers, many (though by no means all) of them poor or on the verge of poverty, one group of feminist scholars has—intentionally or not—ended up justifying, excusing, and in some cases promoting unwed parenthood for young teenage girls. One of the more recent and important of these, Kristen Luker's *Dubious Conceptions: Of the Politics of Teenage Pregnancy*[1] stands as a striking example of a refusal to acknowledge the destructive consequences of teen parenting—and the fatherlessness that most often accompanies it nowadays—for young children, for the babies born to teen mothers, and for the teen mothers themselves.

Collapsing important distinctions between the teen parenting of the past (1940s and 1950s) and the current epidemic of teen illegitimacy, authors such as Luker, Judith Stacey, and others argue that teen pregnancy now is not so much a new thing as a continuation of long-established patterns of reproduction that no one paid much mind to in the "old days" because—and this is treated as a minor matter—most teen mothers were married. Indeed, current teen pregnancy, it often is argued, is not so much a result of young women's careless floundering into bad circumstances (as it was or was thought of in earlier days) but, rather, is a positive, even productive response to the pressures of the environment, particularly economic strains.

Lost in this discussion is the reality of the situation: However problematic teen parenting was in the past, for the most part it meant parenting for two people—mother and father. By contrast, teen parenting today means almost invariably single motherhood for young women who are less likely to be prepared for the complex demands of children than their historical sisters. Why is that? Precisely because the world has changed dramatically and the supporting surround of kith and kin is less likely to be in place. It used to be possible for a young man to support a family with a decent "working-class" job as well. Today this is less and less true. So what, in fact, do we see? Nine out of ten African American teen mothers today are single and the numbers are growing in other communities. The truth is that this tide of teen pregnancy is often a sign of women's powerlessness in sexual encounters in an era where boys are no longer expected to "do the right thing."

Evasion of this issue, in particular the costs to children of teen single parenting, carries grave consequences. To dismiss these in the process of defending the often bad "choices" made by young teenage girls is to perpetuate a downward cycle of reproductive behavior that is good for no one—not for the teen mothers and certainly not for their children. I will explore this evasion through a careful, critical examination of Luker's book as a strong, representative example of the position I oppose. Let me begin on an autobiographical note that will help to mark the difference between an earlier era and the current one.

I was a teenage mother, married, to be sure, but a teenager just the same. I frequently encounter people who find this hard to believe. Teenage motherhood doesn't belong in the same conceptual framework as higher education, book writing, and the professoriat. They are not entirely wrong, even for the era I hail from, when obviously unliberated young men and women "did the right thing" by coupling sex with marriage. A good number of these marriages didn't work out. An astonishing number did. According to Kristin Luker, I was part of the real epidemic, the one that occurred when Eisenhower was in the White House and before the 1960s burst into full flower. Pregnancy was all the rage. The fact that it was preceded by, or tethered to, marriage seems a matter of little moment to Luker. She just notes that society didn't run around having snit fits about teenage pregnancy then because the kids were wed, a matter of diminished import in her view. But today society is hysterical regarding the question, with Democrats and Republicans alike taking aim at the teen mom. To be sure, teen pregnancy is linked to what used to be called "illegitimacy"; to high school dropout rates that are unacceptably high; to dismal or difficult living conditions; to drug and alcohol abuse; and, of course, to more teenage childbearing. The babies of teenage mothers are less likely to flourish than are babies born under more favorable circumstances. They tend to be low-birthweight babies and are less likely to have had adequate prenatal care. All too often, abuse and neglect are malevolent companions on their difficult journey, certainly by comparison to the prospects faced by children born into stable, two-parent situations—the safest environment for children, considering all other alternatives.

This is the picture pointed to by the best available evidence. Luker, however, downplays the overall bleakness of this scenario. One principal figure in the growing teenage mother phenomenon fades to the vanishing point in her discussion, that shadowy entity known as *the baby*. Approximately five pages of consideration in a 283-page book are devoted to babies of unwed teen mothers. Luker's analysis also diverges significantly from the findings summarized in a comprehensive report, "Kids Having Kids," issued by the Robin Hood Foundation, a New York based antipoverty charity—certainly not a stalking-horse for mean and uncaring right-wingers.[2] We learn from this study that adolescent childbearing as an independent factor accounts for a 50 percent lower likelihood of completing high school, 24 percent more children, and 57 percent more time as a single parent during the first thirteen years of parenthood. Luker, by contrast, downplays the deleterious effects of teenage childbearing, resting much of her argument on widely popularized studies done in the early 1990s that haven't borne up very well under stringent empirical examination. Thus, she tilts toward the view that early childbearing should be viewed as a *positive* adaptation to adverse circumstances. Giving birth as a teen is surely a response to circumstances. But to put a positive spin on what is, for the human beings involved, a torn and broken situation, and all too often a disaster, seems shortsighted at best. And it isn't just the lives of the young moms that must concern the responsible researcher. Children born under these circumstances face limited and, in all too many instances, tragedy-limned destinies.

The results of the Robin Hood Foundation report, the most reliable currently available, indicate that young parents, their children, and society all bear the costs of adolescent parenting (to the tune of some extra $6.9 billion a year, more than $2,801 for every teen mother), but that children of teen moms pay the heaviest price of all in poor health, deteriorated home environments, lower cognitive development, worse educational outcomes, higher rates of behavior problems of all kinds, and higher rates of adolescent childbearing. Surprise! Surprise! One wonders how it could be otherwise. It takes heroic effort to raise a child against the odds. The vast majority, unsurprisingly, are not up to it. If you are an unmarried fifteen-year-old kid in a lousy situation, it is difficult to expect heroic action; it is cruel to demand it. So, the home environments for children born to unwed teenage mothers yield double the rate of reported abuse for out-of-wedlock children in general. By the time these kids get to school, they are 40 percent more likely to drop out. Fathers bear relatively little of the costs of adolescent childbearing, for a variety of reasons. Some fathers are unknown to their children, even to the child's mother, if she is sexually active with multiple partners. The disappearance of decent jobs for unskilled workers sufficient to support a family is also a factor—one Luker does emphasize, to her credit.

The United States has the highest rate of unwed, teenage childbearing in the industrial world. The majority of women on welfare began their childbearing as teenagers, and a surprisingly high proportion of incarcerated men were themselves born to teenage mothers—more than 70 percent, according to Sarah S. Brown, director of the National Campaign to Prevent Teen Pregnancy.[3] The upshot, then, is that the effects of teenage childbearing are not negligible to the well-being of the mother, the child, and the wider society. Yet we seem to alternate between extreme responses of two generic varieties. There is the "Lock 'em up and make 'em stop or make 'em pay" school, and then there is the "You don't dare criticize teen pregnancy or you are a moralistic creep who hates sex and besides that the situation isn't so bad or wouldn't be if we just lightened up" camp. Those who discuss this matter from the stump often report on a trump card played in public forums. Let's call it the "clinical veto" move. It works like this. Someone recounts in stirring rhetoric the lives of an unwed mother and child pair who are doing, or have done, very well, thank you. They then become a poster couple for the cause, that cause being general societal support for any choices people make so long as these are *their* choices. If you argue otherwise, you are intolerant and wedded to outmoded ideas. If you offer the riposte that social analysts must look at the overall picture, allowing that individual success stories, however important and edifying, don't change that picture, you are still taken for a mean-spirited sort, one whose veins are not pulsating with appropriate sentimentality.

What does Luker offer to this important debate in our highly charged political atmosphere? Considerably less than one might hope, coming from the author of the distinguished work *Abortion and the Politics of Motherhood*.[4] Perhaps this is because she herself is torn between "hard" social science and a more interpretive method; torn between wanting to support the "rational choices" young, unmarried women make when they get pregnant and keep their babies and recognition that this situation is one fraught with troubles of all sorts; torn between whether this society or any society has a stake in upholding certain norms of social behavior or can, and should, be far more lax in entertaining behaviors of all kinds; torn between articulating desirable limits to sexual activity or embracing the "world of sexual freedom that opened in the 1970s," in which case the mere fact that so many teenagers have sex becomes a prima facie case for teenagers having sex. Whatever is, is normative.

Senator Daniel Patrick Moynihan calls this "defining deviancy down." If illegitimacy has lost its stigma, it is no longer a matter of ethical import. In Luker's words, "in less than a decade a shameful condition was transformed into a personal choice."[5] Notice that the previous situation is always characterized in dire and unattractive terms; the present in words that carry the sheen of our dominant language of consumerism and, increasingly, politics, namely, "choice." And we can no more evaluate these choices—are they good or bad for the persons involved or others—than we can "turn back the clock" on defining deviancy down. "What follows is 'innovative family structures,' namely, single mothers with their children whose lives consist of a series of relationships with noncommitted partners—scarcely partners at all. Luker takes it as a given that sex is "permanently disconnected from marriage." It is this fact, she avers, that has spawned the great anxiety and turned teenagers into scapegoats and targets because they are "participating in the new world of sexual freedom and because most adults are (often rightly) doubtful about the skills and resources these young people possess."[6] Consider the turn of phrase "the new world of sexual freedom." This makes it sound like the final frontier, a zone of free copulation by comparison to the stifling and stifled world of old. The "often rightly" separated off in parentheses is tepid and cautious. The "new world of sexual freedom" is bold and brassy, a marquee glowing and pulsating with the promise of adventure and freshness within.

Luker surely doesn't intend to represent the life of teenage motherhood as a golden possibility—the new freedom, the world of liberation. But her book is of at least two minds. The excerpts from interviews with teenage mothers with which she laces her text are unsettling, showing these kids to be "confused, misinformed, adrift," in her words, as they tell tales of coerced sexual encounters; "doing it" because everybody else was and they were getting teased; finally having sex because they couldn't think of a reason not to but, often, finding it unappealing, not "liking it." Why, then, one wonders, does *Dubious Conceptions* open with an idyll set in a "sunny playroom for toddlers?" A young male child is poised, entranced, "in front of a colorful bead-and-wire toy." His fingers are "chubby." The wires are "bright." A preemie, he is now flourishing after a "rocky start." Across the street, in the high school to which the day care center is attached, the little boy's mother is taking an algebra exam. She wants to be the first member of her family to graduate from high school, and when she does she "has every intention of crossing that auditorium stage three months from now, dressed in her graduation robes and holding baby David in her arms."[7]

This glowing portrait is, by Luker's own admission, anomalous. Teenage mothers are less likely to finish school than are other teens; most do not go on to college; their babies are less likely to flourish. Why, then, begin with a sunny portrait? Luker would respond that she wants to give the problem a "human face." Well and good. But it would be more tough-minded and honest to begin with a far grittier, hence more accurate, representation. Instead we get an urban pastoral with Michelle (her name for the young teen mom) cast as a "pioneer," no less. Why? Because until the mid-1970s, visibly pregnant women were banned from school grounds lest swelling bellies corrupt the minds of youth. But "pioneer" is an odd semantic choice. A pioneer is one who prepares the way for others to follow. Is this territory into which we want more young women to venture? Surely not. That would be irresponsible advocacy. To be sure, there was a good bit of errant nonsense surrounding pregnancy in the old days. I recall that my English teacher in the Cache La Poudre High School in northern Colorado was compelled by school board regulations to leave her job in the middle of the school year once she reached the fourth month of pregnancy and was starting to "show." She was married, of course, but school policy forbade the display of pregnancy to youth—youth who were, by then, sneaking out to see *Rock Around the Clock,* listening to Elvis and the Everlys, mourning the death of Buddy Holly, and figuring out "how far to go" in parked cars on Saturday night. In other words, not quite so shockable as the school board presumed. But sending a married, adult English teacher out of the classroom and into decorous invisibility is not the same thing as exulting in the pioneer achievements of unmarried, pregnant high school girls. Something is wrong with this picture.

To Luker, what is wrong is that conservatives think Michelle is compromising David's future because she is "selfish." Liberals, though kinder (by definition), view Michelle as unwittingly doing harm because she is a victim. She is "too immature to appreciate the implications of her actions." Luker rejects this stance because it denies Michelle "full personhood, exempting her from the obligations of being a moral actor held accountable for the choices she makes."[8] But Luker doesn't consistently uphold accountability, either. In her universe, to assess responsibility is to "blame," and blaming is bad. So we have moral actors without moral responsibility of the sort that presupposes a standard to which others can hold us accountable. This isn't coherent. When pressed, however, Luker retreats behind a defensive perimeter defined by a rigid, extremely narrow social science methodology. We just don't know enough to make any solid judgments. The interpretationist transmogrifies into the narrow positivist who proclaims that you can never endorse or criticize anything in social life unless you can demonstrate beyond dispute an instance of direct linear causation: first x, then y. Does early childbearing really *cause* high school dropouts? Certainly the two phenomena are strongly correlated. But cause and effect? Hmmm. . . . So we'd best demur.

Sure, there is a substantial difference between the "level of education attained by those women who give birth while in junior high or high school and the level attained by those who do not." But: "Is this difference meaningful? Does having a baby truly change a teenager's life in significant ways?"[9] Maybe, maybe not, with the "maybe not" finally winning out because those who become pregnant as teens "differ from other women even before they conceive." Luker returns to this theme again and again, giving the book a quality rather like that of Bill Murray's character in the film *Groundhog Day*, who awakens each morning to his alarm only to find himself yet again in Punxsutawney, Pennsylvania, and it is Groundhog Day. The "here we go again" theme in Luker's volume works like this: Some pretty dismal data are displayed. The misguided use of that data by conservatives, and sometimes by liberals, is remarked upon. The unacceptably narrow approaches of those who stress rational choice too strongly and those who stress victimization too vehemently are lamented. Luker then makes her standard move, one repeated throughout the book: We're really not so sure that the data holds up if what you are looking for is linear causation. So we'd best be agnostic on the outcomes generated by early childbearing because the data isn't unambiguous about the risk factors involved. This is so, according to Luker, because teens who become pregnant are "discouraged" to begin with. If you presume this discouragement as a preexisting factor, the negative effects which appear to "flow" from early sexual experiences and pregnancy likely diminish. These young women were going to have rough lives anyway.

This is a strange argument. It suggests that if a teenager is affluent and has a robust support network, it is okay for her to give birth at age fifteen, a conclusion on which Luker at one point heaps a bit of appropriate scorn yet seems to generalize as the only decent response to the teen mom phenomenon. If only all teen moms had lots of support, especially economic security, we could cease to be anxious and to scapegoat young unmarried women. Thus, unsurprisingly, she situates as the most salient issue in the whole debate the inadequacy of America's medical care system. If a comprehensive system were in place, the health risks to the mother associated with early pregnancy would disappear. Early unwed childbearing is just a fact of modern life. So we'd best acknowledge that and move with all deliberate speed to eliminate poverty, to build better schools and neighborhoods, to create decent jobs for teenage fathers. We also need more and better contraception and abortion, including over-the-counter pill provision without prescription and no questions asked. We need to extend the hours of birth control and abortion clinics. We require highly subsidized day care as part of the public schools ("as in France"). If we do not get this fully gold-plated Total Care System, American society "could conceivably become so punitive and coercive that poor teenagers would be discouraged from ever having babies. . . ." China is cited at this point as a society that "discourages" births the state doesn't want. But what China does is coercive, often brutal, control of its population. This is downplayed as mere "discouragement" in order to make America's future course seem more plausible *unless* certain highly ambitious, comprehensive reforms are undertaken.[10]

Luker folds teenage childbearing into the issue of poverty in order to promote skepticism about whether teenage pregnancy and childbirth correlates "with poverty in any simple way." She puts all her eggs, if you will, into the poverty basket, and concludes that early childbearing doesn't make young women poor; "rather, poverty *makes* women bear children at an early age"[11] [emphasis mine]. Why, one wonders, are we obliged to pick one option or the other? Doesn't it make more sense to look at the ways in which early childbearing deepens and exacerbates other problems? Doesn't it make sense to discourage out-of-wedlock births because they are, in fact, a strong contributing factor to diminished well-being for the mother and a dubious future for the child? Because Luker doesn't do this, by book's end, the agentic dimension she wants to restore to the lives of teen moms has pretty much disappeared. Young women are no longer moral agents. They are flotsam and jetsam on the roiling seas of economic distress: Poverty *makes* them do what they do.

Isn't this the strong assertion of a broad causal claim of the sort Luker cautions against? Luker here, as elsewhere, is at sixes and sevens. She knows there is a problem with too many babies born to too many unmarried moms who are too young. But in her quest to avoid ethical assessment, collapsed, by Luker, into blame, she leaves us nowhere. Her choice of terms commits her tacitly to the view that, if unmarried Michelle is a pioneer, it would seem that we need to encourage, not discourage, her choices. And we can do that only if we, as a society, are willing to pay. Then the problem would no longer be a problem. It is hoped that, with poverty diminished and full-service publicly funded day care available from infancy, with birth control and abortion clinics dotting the landscape and parents prevented from restricting the choices of their teens, more teenagers would "choose" not to have babies. But, one way or the other, with these social reforms and changes, teenage motherhood would no longer be high on our list of social concerns.

For the sake of argument, let's take Luker at her word that, for many a young woman, having a baby is a "pledge of hope," the action of a rational being making the best of an already bad situation. If we are "rightly concerned about how difficult and costly it is to help children like David"—the little boy in the pastoral, remember—then how should we think about Michelle, his mother? Luker is right to remind us that the problem isn't one faced exclusively by African Americans, who comprise about 15 percent of the population of teenage girls but account for more than one-third of teenage mothers, with nine out of ten African American teens who give birth doing so out of wedlock. She is also right to score liberals who presume that the soaring rates of teenage births can be attributed to ignorance and lack of information. They are barking up the wrong tree, according to Luker, for teens certainly know where babies come from. Ignorance is not the issue. So far so good.

Luker then moves to represent the world of the contemporary teen as a universe so different from that inhabited by their parents that a nigh incommensurable gulf exists between the genera-tions—a very American sort of presumption. The "social con-struction model" that shapes her approach leads her to conclude, as well, that all current policy options, whether Republican or Clintonian, must fail because they misdescribe the problem. What, then, is the problem? Well, there are those crabby Puritans, so the problem has deep roots in our history. It used to be the case that people were compelled to get married if the union was about to bear fruit. If things weren't made right, moral pariah status resulted, especially for the woman. That was wrong because it was morally censorious. Nineteenth-century female reformers changed the way we thought about women in trouble by redefin-ing such women as victims of circumstances and runaway male lust rather than as miscreants. The child-saving movement fol-lowed, and with it a concern for "fair play for nameless little ones." In the twentieth century, maladjustment emerged as a goad to precocious sexuality as child advocates and reformers moved in on the scene yet again by demanding and, in most cases, getting compulsory schooling laws; protective labor legislation; the creation of juvenile courts; birth control; and curtailment on the right to marry for "undesirables" like "lunatics, idiots, imbeciles and the feebleminded," a low point in the reformist story. Reform didn't mean control went away; rather, it got redirected.

This quick race through the history of our "construction" of female sexuality and views on childbearing has many interesting moments, but it comes to an abrupt halt with Luker's chastisement of 1970s reformers for their assumption that children born to unwed parents are destined for "a limited and dreary fate," although "there is considerable truth in this assumption."[12] Where, then, do we place the stress? On "considerable truth" or the inaccuracy of assuming that "each and every child" born to an unwed teenage mom puts that child on a course to earthly perdition? Luker here, as elsewhere, is of at least two minds. We know that "children born to unwed parents are more likely to grow up in a single parent home than are children whose parents are married" and "social-science research confirms what most people intuit, [namely, that] children who grow up with a single parent have, on average, fewer of every kind of resource than do children who grow up in two-parent families. . . . Consequently, when we look at the children of unwed parents, we are looking at children who risk having only one parent's love, attention, and income to draw on, and also at children who, because they come from poor families, face independent risks of hardship, whatever their parents' marital status."[13]

This would seem to be reason enough to fret. But Luker takes back much of what she gestures toward. The "legal status" of the parents' relationship is a moot point. Teenage childbearing is a "symptom, not a cause." Her own data, however, suggest that it is both. Why ignore one side of the ledger? Apparently because to do otherwise means one might be called upon to assess more from less desirable behavior; to actually criticize some of the "choices" young women make. That is perilously close to blame for Luker. Throughout the book she veers away from the implications of her own formulae and data. She wants to be an entirely up-to-date person, and it just "isn't realistic to ask today's teens to abstain from sex for a decade or two. . . ."[14] But who is asking that? I haven't heard such espousals from any quarter. But if your alternatives are either sexual freedom or decades of abstention, "sexual freedom" wins the day. And, that being the case, more and better birth control—the whole panoply of reforms noted earlier—kicks in, or would if we were enlightened on this issue. Yet "both liberals and conservatives" in recent years have, harshly and mistakenly, in Luker's view, ascribed the poverty of single moms and babies "to the sexual and reproductive decisions that poor women make." But hold on just a minute. Surely we are not talking about *women*. We are talking about *girls,* adolescents, kids. Are they making decisions in any meaningful sense? When Luker wants to criticize the critics, young women are cast as decision makers. When she wants to goad us into more support for pregnant teenagers, she chides researchers who "assume that people perceive clear choices and [feel] empowered to act on them."[15] It is hard to square these two claims.

About whether to have sex or not, the status of "choice" for teens is murky indeed. Luker's own respondents seem to fall into sexual activity out of conformist pressure or curiosity. It is odd how few mention real sexual desire or excitement. A decision to "keep the baby" surfaces as something akin to a badge of honor and recognition, even if the grandmother is actually raising the child. Luker claims that most teenage moms who carry to term refuse to give up their babies for adoption. This is a shift from an earlier era but, then, "unwed mothers are pioneers on a frontier where increasing numbers of Americans are now settling."[16] And these young women are romantics. That, at least, is Luker's explanation for why girls repudiate the adoption option. They are the beneficiaries of feminist struggle that yielded "hard-won control . . . over fertility," control now "being imperiled" so "all women are having more trouble achieving their fertility preferences." Fertility preferences? Ah, well. So the "fertility preferences" of tens of thousands of teens are to act on their fertility by getting pregnant and keeping the babies because they love them. This makes unwed mothers the true exemplars of "family values." They are repudiating "better material" lives for their children, and that is what adoption is all about. Adoption "means placing more value on cold hard cash than on a young woman's capacity to love."[17] This is grotesque. Rather than seeing adoption as the gift of a loving and stable home to a child, it becomes something akin to baby-selling. Cold hard cash? I know many families who have adopted children. I have two adopted nieces and one adopted nephew. They were adopted because members of my big extended family offered homes and stability and possibility and love that perdures, not an oozy sentiment but a tough-minded commitment to kids who were otherwise destined to rounds of foster care and, in one instance, pariah status, given the nature of her particular cultural circumstances. Why is Luker so keen to stigmatize adoption even as she is avid to avoid criticizing the other practices she describes, practices that she herself concludes contribute to a shopping list of risks for the children of bewildered, disoriented, frustrated, all-at-sea teen moms—and that is an optimistic view. Naive and disoriented young women sometimes can pull it together. Crack- and alcohol-addicted and cognitively limited teenage moms rarely do. The track record here is clear. The resourceful, capable teenage moms are conspicuous by their relative rarity.

Perhaps the most enticing possibility that surfaces in Luker's book is a sideshow, the implications of which she doesn't spell out. She notes that in the days when premarital sex was considered wrong, "young men and women typically negotiated the meaning of each step (the first kiss, the first caress, 'petting') and where it fit into the relationship; the woman permitted increasing sexual intimacy in return for greater commitment from the man. Young women today have no such clear-cut rules."[18] Isn't this another way of saying that young women today—"pioneers" on the frontier of the new freedom—are in fact less powerful in sexual encounters? The process of negotiation has broken down. Teenage girls have lost authoritative negotiating power over intimacy. So the sexual revolution and freedom appears to add up to less real clout for girls. Why must a boy bargain and negotiate and get drawn ever tighter into an orbit of intimacy if he need not? It isn't a matter of boys being boys but teenagers being teenagers and human bodies being human bodies. The girls still face pregnancy. The boys no longer face "doing the right thing." Instead, both have become bereft "pioneers" in what seems a wasteland rather than a garden of delights. But we cannot turn back the clock.

The upshot: What happens to the babies of young, unmarried mothers is a question we are here given leave to evade, go over once lightly, and then to bracket. What happens to our ideas of trust and commitment is a question we don't ask. The implications of a massive defection from the view that sex, marriage, and childbearing have some connection to one another and to basic institutional arrangements, including marriage, is moot. Instead, what is happening empirically—lots of teenage sex; lots of babies at risk being born; lots of teen moms barely coping, frequently collapsing; lots of fathers lost to their children—is just the way we do things around here.

NOTES

1. Kristen Luker, *Dubious Conceptions: Of the Politics of Teenage Pregnancy* (Cambridge, MA: Harvard University Press, 1996).
2. The Robin Hood Foundation, 111 Broadway, 19th floor, New York, N.Y., 10006.

3. National Campaign to Prevent Teen Pregnancy, 2100 M Street, N.W., Suite 300, Washington, D.C., 20037.
4. Kristen Luker, *Abortion and the Politics of Motherhood* (Berkeley, CA: University of California Press, 1984).
5. Luker, *Dubious Conceptions*, p. 97.
6. Ibid., p. 94.
7. Ibid., p. 1.
8. Ibid., p. 4.
9. Ibid., p. 122.
10. Ibid., p. 192.
11. Ibid., p. 192. Emphasis added.
12. Ibid., p. 40.
13. Ibid., p. 40.
14. Ibid., p. 90.
15. Ibid., p. 152.
16. Ibid., p. 135.
17. Ibid., p. 163.
18. Ibid., p. 145-146.

SEVEN

THE ABSENT BLACK FATHER

Dorothy Roberts

WHO IS THE ABSENT FATHER and why has his desertion caused so much alarm? It is impossible to answer these questions without considering absent fathers' racial identity. Even when race is not mentioned, powerful images of promiscuous Black mothers and their shiftless partners shape the debate about fatherlessness. Race influences the reasons people think fatherlessness is a problem and the solutions proposed to address it. If missing fathers are perceived as the cause of society's ills, it is largely because Black culture is considered the benchmark of social degeneracy and female-headed households are the emblem of that culture. It is the absent *Black* father who epitomizes the male component of family breakdown and its deplorable repercussions. Cloaking this depravity in blackness reinforces the opposite family ideal, headed by a breadwinning husband.

This chapter discusses the critical role that absent Black fathers play in the promotion of marital fatherhood as the panacea for children's needs. It does not evaluate the conflicting reports regarding the effects on children of living without a father. It does not determine, for example, whether fatherlessness causes poverty and delinquency, or whether these phenomena are simply tied together by social forces.[1] Rather, it examines how race helps people choose which interpretation to believe. The absent Black father is a main character in the story that says poverty is caused by family form and not by racism or the unequal distribution of wealth, and that reinstating fathers is therefore the solution to poverty.

BLACK MEN AS SYMBOLS OF FATHERLESSNESS

Fatherlessness is seen as a distinctly Black problem. Just as Black single mothers symbolize the threat posed by independent mothering, absent Black fathers represent the dangers of fathering uncivilized by marriage. As historian Gerda Lerner observed, "quite apart from their guilt or innocence, Black men, in particular, are made heroes and villains not by the moral (or immoral) weight of their conscious acts but by the needs of a market that responds to nothing but itself."[2] Making Black men symbols of fatherlessness serves two specific functions: This racial association automatically brands fatherlessness as a depraved condition, and it offers a convenient explanation for Black people's problems.

The female-headed household—not the nuclear family—is the dominant family arrangement for Blacks. Black families have the highest rate of unwed motherhood, with Black families three times as likely as White families to be headed by a woman.[3] Most Black children in the United States are born to unmarried mothers. But the rate among Whites is rising faster. Growing from 3 percent to 25 percent since 1965, the rate of fatherlessness among Whites today has reached what it was among Blacks three decades ago.[4] Today there are more White babies born to single mothers.

Still, single motherhood is viewed as a *Black* cultural trait that is creeping into White homes. "White illegitimacy was generally not perceived as a 'cultural' or racial defect, or as a public expense, so the stigma suffered by the White unwed mother was individual and familial," Rickie Solinger observes in her history of single pregnancy between World War II and *Roe v. Wade*.[5] Black unwed motherhood, on the other hand, was considered a major social problem: "Black women, illegitimately pregnant, were not shamed but simply blamed. . . . There was no redemption possible for these women, only the retribution of sterilization, harassment by welfare officials, and public policies that threatened to starve them." Charles Murray hammered in this point in his *Wall Street Journal* editorial, "The Coming White Underclass," that warns White Americans that their rising illegitimacy rate threatens to spread to White neighborhoods the same crime, drugs, and "drop out from the labor force" that now infects Black communities.[6] It seems only natural for White people to disdain becoming like Blacks. Identifying fatherlessness as a Black trait, then, helps to make this condition seem abnormal and to make the male-centered family seem normal.

The Black family, moreover, has long served as the scapegoat for the Black community's plight and for many of America's ills. Rather than address the effects of centuries of institutionalized deprivation, sociologists have held up family disintegration as the explanation for Black people's failure to achieve success in America. This thesis gained popularity with Daniel Patrick Moynihan's 1965 report, *The Negro Family: The Case for National Action.*[7] Moynihan, then assistant secretary of labor and director of the Office of Policy Planning and Research under President Johnson, described Black culture as a "tangle of pathology" that is "capable of *perpetuating itself* without assistance from the White world." The chief culprit, Moynihan asserted, was Blacks' "matriarchal" family structure. According to Moynihan, "At the heart of the deterioration of the fabric of the Negro society is the deterioration of the Negro family. It is the fundamental cause of the weakness of the Negro community." Under this theory, Black fatherlessness is understood as a symptom of rebellious Black mothering, a symptom that dooms Black people to ruin.

In the discourse about fatherlessness, Black men serve only in negative roles. There is little indication that Black fathers can have any positive effect on their children. Indeed, Black men have never been considered suitable mentors for their children. Slave law installed the White master as the head of an extended plantation family that included his slaves. The plantation family ruled by White slaveholders was considered the best institution to transmit moral precepts to uncivilized Africans.[8] Courts reasoned that the slave-owners' moral authority over the family was ordained by divine imperative. Slaves, on the other hand, had no legal authority over their children. Naming a slave after his owner reinforced the child's ultimate subservience to his White master rather than to his parents.

Emancipation and formal equality have not given Black parents complete control over their children. State child protection departments disproportionately remove Black children from their homes, welfare programs restructure Black families as a condition of receiving benefits, and government bureaucrats supervise Black parents who fall under their jurisdiction. Malcolm X, describing the disruption of his own family by child welfare workers, noted the contemporary parallels to slavery: "A Judge . . . had authority over me and all of my brothers and sisters. We were 'state children,' court wards; he had the full say-so over us. A White man in charge of a Black man's children! Nothing but legal, modern slavery. . . ."[9] My point is not that Black men should be entitled to dominate their families as White men have but that they have never been entitled to do so.

Black men were depicted as menacing brutes or ridiculous buffoons, disparaging images that justified their exclusion from citizenship early in this nation's history.[10] The Black men portrayed in the media and on the minds of many Americans today—gangster rappers, hustlers, rapists, gang bangers, drug dealers, crack heads—are no more virtuous. In short, Black men are not supposed to be role models for their children. Some commentators believe that the hypersexual and violent Black man needs the taming influence of marriage more than anyone. But in their rhetoric, he is someone to be disciplined, not given power or respect.

Certainly White Americans do not expect Black men to occupy the position White men have held, to finally extinguish the image of "black men as simple-minded pretenders to the throne of White masculine nobility."[11] This is why we cannot see the fatherhood movement only as a patriarchal campaign to reinstate husbands to their rightful place as rulers of their families. The last thing most White Americans want is to amplify *Black* males' masculinity. Black men represent all of the negative aspects of fatherlessness but none of the positive potential of fatherhood.

CREATING THE ABSENT BLACK FATHER

While Black fathers are disparaged for their absence, a number of societal forces work to discourage their family participation. The reasons for the high rate of Black single motherhood are the subject of intense controversy. Some conservative commentators, such as Charles Murray, William Bennett, and Mickey Kaus, argue that the promise of welfare benefits induces childbearing out of wedlock.[12] (Numerous studies have refuted this claim.) Some Black feminists, such as Regina Austin and Barbara Omolade, point to a positive cultural tradition that is more accepting of unmarried mothers.[13] I, too, have suggested that we might view Black single mothers as resistors against patriarchy.[14] But the liberatory potential of mothering outside the nuclear family model does not discount the historical disruption of Black families. The effects of racial repression, most notably high rates of unemployment and incarceration, continue to contribute to Black fathers' absence from the home.

Chronic poverty is not conducive to forming stable marriages. For better or worse, women are less likely to marry or otherwise stick with men who offer little financial advantage. The stresses and dislocations caused by unemployment make sustained partnership difficult. Black sociologist William Julius Wilson, among others, makes a convincing case that the rise in

Black female-headed households is directly tied to Black male joblessness.[15] Black men's unemployment rates are more than double those of White men, and in 1988, there were more Black women in the labor force than Black men.[16] Black men's declining ability to contribute financially to their households is a major cause of fatherlessness in Black homes. Wilson mistakenly focused his reforms on empowering Black men alone, accepting the premise that family structure causes poverty and advocating rebuilding the traditional family as a key to solving Black poverty. Yet he is most certainly correct in predicting that improving Black men's economic status would increase the numbers who live with their children.

Black fathers also are separated from their families by imprisonment. Blacks, mostly men, make up over half of the one million inmates in American jails. The racial disparity in incarceration rates continues to rise, with nearly eight Blacks in state and federal prisons in 1994 for every White person incarcerated.[17] In some cities, huge portions of the Black male population are under supervision of the criminal justice system—awaiting trial, in prison, or on probation or parole. A 1991 study found that in Baltimore, Maryland, for example, 56 percent of the Black males between the ages of eighteen and thirty-five were being so monitored on any given day.[18] The numbers in Washington, D.C., are similar.[19] These appalling incarceration rates stem not only from the disproportionate poverty and desperation that plagues Black communities but also from federal and state sentencing policies that are tougher on Black drug offenders.[20] Locking a man up essentially makes him ineligible for marriage, rips him away from his family, and prevents him from providing financial support. Ex-convicts have a hard time finding a decent job, which makes it difficult for them ever to become the ideal father.

Black men do not value family relationships any less than other men do. But many have been restrained by unemployment, imprisonment, and other deprivations from developing the family ties they desire.

RACE, MARRIAGE, AND THE MEANING OF THE GOOD FATHER

Despite these forces that degrade Black fathers both materially and figuratively, these men play a critical role in defining the good father. The absent Black father stands in contradistinction to the ideal of father as breadwinning husband. Under nineteenth-century separate spheres ideology, which applied only to White families, the husband sustained the family economically and represented the family in the public arena, while the wife cared for the private realm of the home.[21] Despite the material benefits that accrued from their household labor, housewives were rendered economically dependent on their husbands. Although the number of wage-earning women has increased dramatically, those who are not tied to a wage-earning husband are stigmatized, denied many social benefits, and more likely to live in poverty.[22] A contemporary television commercial for a mortgage company portrays a man boasting "My wife thinks I'm perfect because I make sure all the bills are paid on time." Paying the bills continues to be the measure of the perfect father.

The separate spheres ideology excluded Black women, however, who were always expected to work outside their homes.[23] The image of the Black matriarch similarly violated the ideal of the dependent mother. Black men also fail to fit the patriarchal model of the husband who sustains his family economically.

Labeling a child "fatherless" usually means that the parents are not married. "Fatherlessness" is often used interchangeably with "single motherhood" or "illegitimacy." Leading fatherhood advocate David Blankenhorn asserts that "*[m]arried* fatherhood is a socializing role for men."[24] He includes among "fatherless" children those who live with stepfathers or who spend half their time with their divorced fathers in joint custody arrangements. Critics seem far more concerned with castigating unmarried fathers than with examining the actual contributions of married fathers to their children's well-being. Blankenhorn even ridicules the "New

Father" who is nurturing and emotionally involved with his kids for not being masculine enough. Given the continued expectation that mothers will serve as the primary caretakers of their children, the idealized role of father has little to do with men's involvement with their children. Thus, it is a man's failure to marry or remain married to the mother that is supposed to create the problems linked to fatherlessness.

Further evidence of this understanding of fatherlessness is the distinction made by the welfare system between children whose mothers become widowed and children whose mothers never marry or get divorced.[25] The former are not stigmatized at all and receive survivors' benefits through Social Security—the most generous type of public assistance paid to mothers. The latter are more likely to receive Aid to Families with Dependent Children (AFDC) benefits, which are both disparaged and meager. This helps to explain why the poverty rate among widows is half that of single mothers on welfare.[26] This distinction between widows and welfare mothers parallels the stratification of the American welfare system into two basic categories— social insurance and what is commonly called "welfare." Social insurance (Social Security and unemployment insurance) provides dignified entitlement to wage-earners and their spouses and children, whereas welfare (mainly AFDC) doles out humiliating, undeserved relief to poor single mothers.[27] Social Security retains its political popularity because it is perceived as an insurance program despite its strong redistributive effects and its dependent clients. Taxpayers complain about supporting "fatherless" children on AFDC but not the children of deceased male workers.

The categorization of welfare is both gendered and racialized. Entitlement is determined by the nature of the mother's relationship to a man—whether she was married to a wage-earner or not. As welfare rights activist Theresa Funiciello points out, "[t]he only real difference between 'survivor' families and 'welfare' families . . . is the imprimatur of the father."[28] Moreover, Black single mothers make up a disproportionate share of AFDC recipients, while a smaller percentage of Black widows than White widows receive the preferred survivors' insurance. White mothers are much more likely to be married and to be married to a man who earns enough to ensure survivors' benefits.

While critics of fatherlessness focus on marriage statistics, little attention is paid to the actual involvement of Black men in the lives of their children. Nor has there been much investigation of the extent of male mentoring in the Black community, provided by grandfathers, uncles, older half brothers, church elders, and neighbors, as well as fathers. Black sociologists and feminists have noted Black mothers' creative departure from the nuclear family model. Black mothers have a long-standing cultural tradition of sharing child raising with other women in the community.[29] These cooperative networks include members of the extended family (grandmothers, sisters, aunts, and cousins) as well as nonblood kin and neighbors. Patricia Hill Collins uses the term "othermothers" to describe the women who help biological mothers by sharing mothering responsibilities.[30]

This practice, which helps Black mothers overcome the stresses and strains of single parenting, suggests that many of the negative claims about fatherlessness do not apply to Black folks. Just as Black women have a distinct notion of motherhood, so Black men have their own style of fathering. Similar attention to Black fathering would reveal that many presumably "absent" Black fathers actually play an important role in child rearing. Many Black men stay closely tied to their children even when they are not married to the mother or are unable to provide financial support.[31] Stephanie Coontz reports that in one national study "poor African-American, officially absent fathers actually had *more* contact with their children and gave them more informal support than did White, middle-class absent fathers."[32] Indeed, if we want to imagine nurturing fatherhood, decoupled from the patriarchal economic model, we might begin by looking to Black fathers.

FATHERLESSNESS AND WELFARE POLICY

What condemns the absent Black father, then, is not his lack of involvement with his children but his marital and economic status. A good father is a married breadwinner. And Black men typically have not fit that role. Trying to live up to this mainstream ideal historically has been the source of internal turmoil within Black families.[33] The economic definition of father has excluded the Black family from society's respect and support, as well. It has branded Black men as irresponsible fathers and justified a stingy welfare system that disadvantaged Black families from the outset.[34] The absent Black father is the antithesis of the ideal of the wage-earning husband. His frightening image bolsters the patriarchal paradigm, which, in turn, justifies preserving a social order that has consigned generations of Black children to poverty.

For decades, welfare policy forced Black men out of the home. Since welfare's inception, states have conditioned payments on mothers' compliance with standards of sexual and reproductive morality, such as "suitable-home" rules.[35] During the 1960s, at the time when Black women finally secured entitlements to AFDC benefits, eligibility became increasingly burdened with such requirements. Many states granted aid only if a parent of the needy child was continually absent from the home, denying payments if the child's father or "substitute father" lived there. This "man-in-the-house" regulation penalized poor children of "nonabsent" fathers by denying them welfare benefits. The result was to throw thousands of children off the roles (in Alabama, the number of AFDC recipients declined by 22 percent) and thousands of fathers out of their homes.[36]

Today the trend has reversed: New welfare laws attempt to reinstate absent Black fathers. In the three years before Congress passed the 1996 welfare reform law, at least thirty states applied for federal waivers allowing them to change their welfare programs to incorporate a form of behavior modification.[37] Two of the most popular reforms are rules that require welfare mothers to undergo mandatory paternity proceedings and that encourage them to get married.

New welfare programs that penalize poor Black mothers for failing to marry only worsen their families' welfare. It is especially unlikely that marriage or child support will eradicate the poverty of most Black children. Research suggests that there are racial differences in paths to poverty for women. Whereas many White women are left impoverished by divorce, Black single mothers are more likely to be the victims of "reshuffled poverty," caused by the dissolution of a poor two-parent household.[38] While about half of poor White single mothers became poor at the time they established a single-mother household, only a quarter of Black women did-the Black mothers were already poor before the separation. A study of children's poverty concluded that "[f]amily structure patterns are more powerful determinants of the economic fates of White than Black children."[39] Because marital breakdown is unlikely to be the cause of Black children's poverty, marriage is unlikely to be the solution.

Collecting child support from fathers will be no more successful than marriage at ending children's poverty. Since 1975 Congress has enacted increasingly tough measures designed to recoup welfare costs by collecting child support.[40] Yet intensified state and federal campaigns to improve child support collection have failed either to lower the poverty rate for children or to reduce significantly the number of children on welfare. The Department of Health and Human Services projects that higher child support payments would enable less than 10 percent of families on welfare to rise above the poverty level.[41]

No matter how vigorously enforced, a child support order cannot raise the earnings of a low-income or unemployed father. Again, relying on paternal child support penalizes Black children because Black fathers are less likely to earn the wages necessary to ensure adequate support for their children. Policies that replace welfare with child support collection, therefore, tend to benefit White children and disadvantage Black children. Researchers calculated, for example, that under Wisconsin's percentage of income child support formula, White families obtained a $481 million annual gain whereas Black and Hispanic families suffered more than a $200 million loss.[42]

Ironically, compelled paternity proceedings may *increase* rather than reduce the number of absent Black fathers. In some cases, child support orders lead to undesired contact with fathers; but, in others, they may force poor fathers to go underground. As law professor and child support expert David Chambers notes, "some of these unemployed and marginally unemployable men who are not supporting their children have informal relationships with their children that the mothers applaud and that might be lost if they are turned into fugitives."[43] In short, while the state should help mothers to collect child support from fathers who can pay it, it is ludicrous to believe that child support can relieve most Black children's poverty.

Even if marriage would improve poor mothers' financial well-being, this result would not justify affirmatively linking their economic options to marriage. But this is precisely the effect of "bridefare" programs that give mothers monetary rewards for marrying. The New Jersey Family Development Act, for example, allows families to earn income up to 150 percent of the poverty-line income and still keep their AFDC benefits, Medicaid, and emergency housing assistance if, and only if, the mother marries.[44] This means that a woman with two children who marries can keep her children's AFDC benefits as well as up to $21,000 of earned income per year.[45] The law's primary sponsor, Assemblyman Wayne Bryant, hoped to entice Black welfare mothers into replicating a middle-class family structure.

The bridefare provision, however, denies this "income disregard" to an unmarried woman who lives with the working father of her children, to a working mother who does not have a husband, and to two mothers who decide to pool their resources to support their children in a single household. Although Bryant claimed the law was designed to teach welfare mothers "to become successful, responsible, and self-sufficient in our society," he clearly was more interested in women's marital status than their financial independence. In fact, bridefare privileges nonworking welfare mothers who rely on a husband's salary over independent, wage-earning mothers on welfare. Measures like the one in New Jersey do not tie welfare to marriage in order to end children's poverty. They tie welfare to marriage in order to champion the traditional, husband-headed family and thereby penalize single, rebellious Black mothers.

Race connects the fatherlessness campaign to welfare reform in a more fundamental way. Alarm over fatherlessness masks the shameful facts about Black Americans' economic status. In reality, the correlation between *race* and poverty overshadows the correlation between *fatherlessness* and poverty. A Black child whose father is present still is likely to fare worse than a White child raised by a single mother.[46] In other words, racial inequality—not fatherlessness—is the leading cause of Black children's deprivation. Pretending that Black poverty is the fault of absent Black fathers provides a defense against addressing America's institutionalized racism.

A majority of Americans have rejected a generous and just system of social provision largely because of its association with poor Black mothers.[47] They are unwilling to spend their tax dollars on programs believed to benefit primarily Black children and that threaten to erode their racial privilege. Reinstating the absent father has become the substitute for a strong welfare state. This movement focuses attention on private causes and solutions to children's poverty, eliminating the need to create a more egalitarian system. In this way, the absent Black father affects policies with repercussions far beyond the Black family.

The diatribe about Black fatherlessness serves far more to discipline Black men and women than to improve the lives of Black children. It pretends that half of Black children are born into poverty because their fathers are not around, not because their fathers are jobless. It lets America off the hook for failing to construct a system of welfare (in the broad sense) that ensures the well-being of all its citizens. It is part of the age-old trick of convincing people that the problems of disempowered groups result from their own bad habits and not from an unequal social structure. But attempts to manipulate the Black family are no substitute for economic and political justice. We cannot begin to judge Black fathers until we address the institutional forces that keep marriage a patriarchal system, devalue the work of child rearing, and deprive families of the social resources necessary to raise healthy children.

NOTES

Thanks to Decanda Faulk for her excellent research assistance.

1. For a refutation of negative claims about fatherlessness, see Nancy E. Dowd, *In Defense of Single-Parent Families* (New York: New York University Press, 1997).

2. Quoted in Paula Giddings, "The New Season/Art: Black Males and the Prison Myth," *New York Times*, September 11, 1994, B50.

3. Carrie Teegardin, "Single with Children," *Atlanta Journal and Constitution*, May 7, 1995, 6G.

4. Lee Smith, "The New Wave of Illegitimacy," *Fortune*, April 18, 1994, 81; Tamar Lewin, "Creating Fathers Out of Men with Children," *New York Times*, June 18, 1995, A1.

5. Rickie Solinger, *Wake Up Little Susie: Single Pregnancy and Race Before Roe v. Wade* (New York: Routledge, 1992), pp. 24-25.

6. Charles Murray, "The Coming White Underclass," *Wall Street Journal*, October 29, 1993, A14.

7. Daniel P. Moynihan, Office of Planning & Policy Research, U.S. Department of Labor, *The Negro Family: The Case for National Action* (1965), p. 4, 5, 29.

8. Orlando Patterson, *Slavery and Social Death: A Comparative Study* (Cambridge, MA: Harvard University Press, 1982), 189-190; Margaret A. Burnham, "An Impossible Marriage: Slave Law and Family Law," *Law and Inequality* 5 (1987), 187, 194.

9. Malcolm X, Alex Haley, *The Autobiography of Malcolm X* (New York: Grove, 1965), 21-22.

10. Ronald I. Takaki, *Iron Cages: Race and Culture in Nineteenth-Century America* (New York: Knopf, 1979).

11. Giddings, "Black Males and the Prison Myth," 50.

12. Charles Murray, *Losing Ground: American Social Policy, 1950-1980* (New York: Basic Books, 1984), 154-166; William J. Bennett, "The Best Welfare Reform: End It," *Washington Post,* March 30, 1994, A19; Mickey Kaus, *The End of Equality* (New York: Basic Books, 1992).

13. Regina Austin, "Sapphire Bound," *Wisconsin Law Review* (1989), 539; Barbara Omolade, "The Unbroken Circle: A Historical and Contemporary Study of Black Single Mothers and Their Families," *Wisconsin Women's Law Journal* 3 (1987), 239.

14. Dorothy E. Roberts, "Racism and Patriarchy in the Meaning of Motherhood," in Martha A. Fineman and Isabel Karpin (eds.), *Mothers in Law: Feminist Theory and the Legal Regulation of Motherhood* (New York: Columbia University Press, 1995), 224, 238.

15. William Julius Wilson, *The Truly Disadvantaged: The Inner City, The Underclass, and Public Policy* (Chicago: University of Chicago Press, 1987); William Julius Wilson, *When Work Disappears: The World of the New Urban Poor* (New York: Knopf, 1996).

16. Theresa Amott and Julie Matthaei, "We Specialize in the Wholly Impossible: African American Women," in Theresa Amott & Julie Matthaei, *Race, Gender, and Work: A Multi-Cultural Economic History of Women in the United States* (Boston, MA: South End Press, 1991), 141, 181.

17. Fox Butterfield, "Many Black Men Barred from Voting," *New York Times,* January 30, 1997, A12.

18. National Center on Institutions and Alternatives, *Hobbling a Generation: Young African American Males in the Criminal Justice System of America's Cities, Baltimore, Maryland* (Alexandria, VA: National Center on Institutions and Alternatives, 1992). On the criminal justice system's disproportional supervision of young Black men, see generally Jerome G. Miller, *Search and Destroy: African-American Males in the Criminal Justice System* (New York: Cambridge University Press, 1996).

19. Jerome G. Miller, *Hobbling a Generation: Young African American Males in Washington, D.C.'s Criminal Justice System* (Washington, DC: National Center on Institutions and Alternatives, 1992), 1.

20. Michael Tonry, *Malign Neglect: Race, Crime, and Punishment in America* (New York: Oxford University Press, 1995).

21. See Nancy F. Cott, *The Bonds of Womanhood: "Women's Sphere" in New England, 1780-1835* (New Haven, CT: Yale University Press, 1977); Frances E. Olsen, "The Family and The Market: A Study of Ideology and Legal Reform," *Harvard Law Review* 96 (1983), 1497, 1498-1501.

22. Martha A. Fineman, *The Neutered Mother, The Sexual Family, and Other Twentieth Century Tragedies* (New York: Routledge, 1995).

23. See Jacqueline Jones, *Labor of Love, Labor of Sorrow: Black Women, Work and the Family from Slavery to the Present* (New York: Basic Books, 1985).

24. David Blankenhorn, "The State of the Family and the Family Policy Debate," *Santa Clara Law Review* 36 (1996): 431, 433. See also David Blankenhorn, *Fatherless America: Confronting Our Most Urgent Social Problem* (New York: Basic Books, 1995).

25. Dorothy E. Roberts, "Irrationality and Sacrifice in the Welfare Reform Consensus," *Virginia Law Review* 81 (1995): 2607.

26. Dowd, *In Defense of Single-Parent Families,* 23.

27. Linda Gordon, *Pitied But Not Entitled: Single Mothers and the History of Welfare* (New York: Free Press, 1994) 1-6; Joel F. Handler and Yeheskel Hasenfeld, *The Moral Construction of Poverty: Welfare Reform in America* (Newbury Park, CA: Sage Publications, 1991).

28. Theresa Funiciello, *Tyranny of Kindness: Dismantling the Welfare System to End Poverty in America* (New York: Atlantic Monthly Press, 1993), 9.

29. Carol Stack, *All Our Kin: Strategies for Survival in a Black Community* (New York: Harper Collins, 1974).

30. Patricia H. Collins, "The Meaning of Motherhood in Black Culture and Black Mother/Daughter Relationships," *Sage* 4 (1987): 3, 5.

31. Dowd, *In Defense of Single Parents,* 107; Robert Joseph Taylor, Linda M. Chatters, M. Belinda Tucker, and Edith Lewis, "Developments in Research on Black Families: A Decade of Review," *Journal of Marriage and the Family* 52 (1990), 993, 996, and 1001.

32. Stephanie Coontz, *The Way We Never Were: American Families and the Nostalgia Trap* (New York: Basic Books, 1992), 248.

33. Ibid, 250.

34. See Gordon, *Pitied But Not Entitled;* Dorothy E. Roberts, "Welfare and the Problem of Black Citizenship," *Yale Law Journal* 105 (1996), 1563.

35. Gordon, *Pitied But Not Entitled,* 45-47; Mimi Abromovitz, *Regulating the Lives of Women: Social Welfare Policy from Colonial Times to the Present* (Boston: South End Press, 1988), 323-26; Winifred Bell, *Aid to Dependent Children* (New York: Columbia University Press, 1965), 29-136.

36. See *King v. Smith,* 392 U.S. 309 (1968) (invalidating Alabama's "substitute father" regulation).

37. See Susan Bennett and Kathleen A. Sullivan, "Disentitling the Poor: Waivers and Welfare Reform," *University of Michigan Journal of Law Reform* 26 (1993), 741, 742; Lucy A. Williams, "The Ideology of Division: Behavior Modification Welfare Reform Proposals," *Yale Law Journal* 102 (1992), 719, 723-24.

38. Mary Jo Bane, "Household Composition and Poverty: Which Comes First?," in Sheldon H. Danziger and Daniel H. Weinberg (eds.), *Fighting Poverty: What Works and What Doesn't* (Cambridge, MA: Harvard University Press), 227-28, 231 table 9.6.

39. Greg J. Duncan and Willard Rodgers, "Longitudinal Aspects of Children's Poverty," *Journal of Marriage and Family* 50 (1988), 1007, 1012.

40. Andrea H. Beller and John W. Graham, *Small Change: The Economics of Child Support* (New Haven, CT: Yale University Press, 1993).

41. Johanna Brenner, "Towards a Feminist Perspective on Welfare Reform," *Yale Journal of Law and Feminism* 2 (1989): 99, 123.

42. Irwin Garfinkel, Daniel R. Meyer & Gary D. Sandefur, "The Effects of Alternative Child Support Systems on Blacks, Hispanics, and Non-Hispanic Whites," *Social Service Review* 66 (1992): 505, 518 table 3.

43. David Chambers, "Fathers, the Welfare System, and the Virtues and Perils of Child Support Enforcement," *Virginia Law Review* 81 (1995), 2575, 2597.

44. Nina Perales, "A 'Tangle of Pathology': Racial Myth and the New Jersey Family Development Act," in Fineman and Karpin, *Mothers in Law,* 252-53.

45. Ibid.

46. Sara McLanahan and Gary Sandefur, *Growing Up with a Single Parent: What Hurts, What Helps* (Cambridge, MA: Harvard University Press, 1994), 85: "It is important to remember that Black children in two-parent families have much higher poverty rates than white children in single-parent families. Hence, if there were no single-parent families, Black children would still have much higher poverty rates than white children."

47. Roberts, "Welfare and the Problem of Black Citizenship"; Jill Quadagno, *The Color of Welfare: How Racism Undermined the War on Poverty* (New York: Oxford University Press, 1994).

EIGHT

FATHER HUNGER

Maggie Gallagher

INCREASINGLY IN AMERICA children are being raised by women alone. Men bear less and less responsibility—financial, emotional, and logistical—for the children they have helped create. This is the context in which fatherhood is now being raised as an issue, not just by men who feel marginalized or shut out from family life, but by mothers abandoned by mates, by young women increasingly anxious about the direction of their future lives, and, above all, by children of divorce grown large enough to speak about their own experiences.

In a speech on June 7, 1997, before the Congress of American Family and conciliation courts, Judith Wallerstein released results of interviews, some of these from children of divorce, now in their late twenties and early thirties, whom she had been following for twenty-five years.[1] Wallerstein's sample is not representative. Instead it represents in some sense the cream of the divorce crop: kids of relatively affluent, well-educated parents raised in the security of Northern California suburbs. At eighteen, she points out, child support ended and these kids were expected to support themselves. One-third of these kids ended up with only a high school diploma. Only 6 of the 130 kids received full support from parents (and stepparents) for higher education. All 6 held good jobs in good professions. The rest struggled to work and complete schooling and wound up in occupations "below" that of their parents.

All of these adult children of divorce were, in Wallerstein's words, "apprehensive about marriage," voicing the sentiment that "Love with sexual intimacy is a strange thing to me." Or, as one participant said, "I can't date, because I can't marry."[2] Already they worried about the effect of divorce on their as-yet unconceived children.

Her conclusion? "Adults get over the divorce, but unlike adults, children's suffering doesn't reach a peak at divorce." Instead "the impact of the divorce increases over time—throughout the first three decades of life."[3]

From an adult point of view the problems raised by a 50 percent divorce rate and a 30 percent out-of-wedlock birth rate may appear manageable. At least, if we celebrate unfettered choice as the highest possible good, the costs to adults of this new burst of family diversity may dwindle compared to the one great benefit: maximizing options.

When we choose to look at family fragmentation from the point of view of the child, a very different picture emerges. For one thing, children have no choice in the matter, and very little voice. As Barbara Dafoe Whitehead points out in her new book, *The Divorce Culture,* the chatter in the chattering classes tends to portray adults as emotionally fragile and therefore needing divorce to escape the strains of marital difficulty, while children are portrayed as emotionally resilient and therefore able to overcome easily the strains produced by divorce.[4]

The real problem, from the child's point of view, is not just "fatherlessness" but father abandonment; not simply the absence of fathers in the home but the presence somewhere close by of a father who does not seem to care.

This was the theory, the happy theory: Every day in every way fathers are getting better and better.

"Until recently," as two eminent family scholars optimistically maintain, "a father could feel he was fulfilling his parental obligations merely by supporting his family. . . . Today, however, the role of father is beginning to demand much more active involvement in the life of the family, especially with regard to child rearing."[5]

". . . [A]n increasing number of men are now taking the primary responsibility for child rearing or are sharing equally," agreed a psychologist in a popular advice book.[6]

This is the reality, the sad reality: Jason is a well-loved nine-year-old tousled blond boy, who laughs easily and chatters with adults. He lives with his mother, Lori. His dad lives fifteen minutes away, but he almost never sees him.

"He's okay," says Jason, swatting away a tear, "I don't know when he's telling the truth or when he's actually going to show up."

Lori, a loving, affectionate mother, is worried. Jason appears a normal, well-adjusted kid. But once in a while he tells his mother he wants to kill himself. "Issues of potential loss affect him deeply," she says. "I've been dating a guy for one week and he already wants me to marry him and make him his daddy."[7]

I know what she's talking about.

It's an ache in the heart, a gnawing anxiety in the gut. It's a longing for a man, not just a woman, who will care for you, protect you, and show you how to survive in the world. For a boy, especially, it's the raw, persistent, desperate hunger for dependable male love, and for an image of maleness that is not at odds with love.

Father hunger.

The signs of it are everywhere, if you know what to look for. I saw it first in my own son's six-year-old eyes as he watched, riveted to the screen, the phenomenally successful *Teenage Mutant Ninja Turtles*. Homeless, born of radioactive goo, the valiant turtles, nurtured and instructed by their surrogate father, a giant ninja-master rat, must save a city and a boy from the ravages of the predatory male: Shredder.

The dramatic tension is created by the boy's need to choose between moral poles: Will he accept the authority of the good dad or lures of the evil one? The home or the gang? The father or the fascist?

"I am your father," Shredder hypnotically booms at the gang of teen boys he has assembled.

"You call this a family?" one of the heroes replies scornfully. And in the end: "All fathers love their children," the Rat-guru reassures the troubled boy, who then rejects the gang and reunites with his own father.

Father hunger is a riff that runs through TV culture in the 1980s and 1990s, producing a sudden explosion of unlikely families in which a perplexing multiplicity of loving fathers care for motherless children. *Full House,* in which three adorably blond little girls are raised by three loving and affectionate men: their dad, his dead wife's brother, and his best friend; *My Two Dads,* in which two men are so determined to be great dads that, despite their uncertainty as to which of them is actually the father, they agree to raise the little girl together.

It's emerged even more clearly as a major theme in motion pictures aimed at boys: in sports films such as the wildly popular *Mighty Ducks,* in which the boy finds in his coach a kind of surrogate father and tries to get him interested in his single mother, and even more obviously in films like 1994's *Getting Even with Dad*—in which a clever but sad young boy blackmails his divorced father into spending time with him and in the end makes his dad fall in love with him again. And the summer of 1994's hit, *Angels in the Outfield,* which begins when a boy wistfully asks his drop-in dad, "When are we going to be a real family again?" "I'd say when the Angels win the pennant," his father replies scornfully, before zipping off on his motorcycle.

These are modern fairy tales in which the wickedly absent father is replaced by a warmly loving father figure, or even transformed by the attractions of a child and the love of a good woman into the devoted dad of every kid's dreams.

Celluloid fathers like these, raised up by entrepreneurs, quick to spot unfulfilled appetites, are only one response to our children's hunger. Evidence of father hunger offscreen is no less dramatic.

The end of marriage entails many losses for children. Of these, the most intensely painful and enduring—and the most common—is the loss of the father.

The first way fathers are lost is physically. Therapists may reassure children that "though Mommy and Daddy don't love each other anymore, they will always love you," but children of divorce know better. For most children of divorce, domicile is destiny: Only one-third of all children living apart from their fathers get to see their dads as often as once a week.[8]

For the first year or so, fathers make a special effort to see their children. As life goes on, as they or the children move inconvenient distances away, or as they acquire additional emotional obligations to new wives or girlfriends with stepchildren or new babies, or as the crisis subsides and the children seem to be getting on fine, or as men grow weary of facing continual hostility from ex-wives, or for a hundred other reasons or no reason—fathers' contact with their children dwindles rapidly. Ten years down the road, two-thirds of all children of divorce have virtually no contact with their fathers.[9] As four distinguished researchers concluded, "[M]arital dissolution typically involves either a complete cessation of contact between the nonresidential parent and child or a relationship that is tantamount to a ritual form of parenthood. . . ."[10]

Children whose parents fail to marry in the first place have even less dependable connections to their fathers.[11] Outside of marriage, the same pattern of the disappearing dad emerges. On average, the child born outside of marriage spends just six months living with his or her father. According to a study conducted by Robert I. Lerman, an economics professor at American University, three-fifths of unwed fathers whose children are age two or younger see their kids regularly. But by the time the kids reach the age of seven and a half, less than a quarter of fathers still see their children frequently.[12] Altogether, as University of Pennsylvania researchers concluded after one large-scale survey of children of single parents, "Fathers, in particular, were more likely not to have had any contact at all than to have seen their children even once in the past twelve months."[13]

Put the divorce and illegitimacy statistics together and you come up with this disturbing trend: A baby born today stands a roughly fifty-fifty chance of keeping his or her father. Previous generations lost fathers to the grave, but this is the first generation of Americans for whom paternal abandonment has become the norm. This is the first generation of American kids who must face not the sad loss of death but the brutal knowledge that other things are far more important to their fathers than they are.

Father hunger is the bane of single mothers everywhere, who often find to their surprise that not all love is personal, rational, and based on intimate acquaintanceship. Penelope Rowlands, a never-married San Francisco magazine writer with a five-year-old son, was shocked by it: "My son began asking for his father before he was two. I'll never forget it. He said, 'Why no daddy?'"[14]

Bonnie is forty-five with light-brown wavy hair, large eyes with big circles under them, a teacher of deaf children and the never-married mother of eight-year-old Michael. She, too, knows about father hunger. Bonnie and baby Michael had lived in Germany for seven months. Then, feeling she needed a family, she came back to the United States and lived with her mother. "At first I went to every family gathering. I put a lot of emphasis on getting him together with his cousins and aunts and uncles. But still, even with all these people around him, I realized it's not the same. Something was missing. There's this hole."

This hole is in Michael's heart. Now eight years old, he has seen his dad only on a few visits, here and in Germany. His father pays no support, but he tells Bonnie he will send money for airplane tickets "any time." In the past, Bonnie has taken Michael to Germany to visit his dad. Because she has very little money, they both have to stay in his dad's apartment. When they do so, Michael tries to make his mom and dad hold hands.

This year, Michael is mad at Bonnie, for she refuses to take him to Germany. "It's too painful," Bonnie says.

What's too painful? Seeing how much her son loves his father, even though his father does nothing for him, and even though he is carelessly cruel in his disregard to her.

This is not an uncommon circumstance: "Most children do not give up on their fathers, even if they are ne'er-do-wells who have abandoned them without a backward glance . . . ," notes Judith Wallerstein. "[C]hildren turn around and construct a credible image of the father they never knew from any scraps of information that they can collect and tend to idealize him in the process."[15]

Therapists tell mothers like Bonnie that they shouldn't interfere with this idealization process, and, looked at cold-bloodedly in the light of reason and the best interests of the child, they are right.

But whose blood is that cold? Certainly not Bonnie's, for whom Michael is not just her child but her whole family, her great love and ruling passion. She is not a particularly angry person, and she has tried very hard not to let her feelings interfere with Michael's well-being. But still the man Michael loves and longs for is the man who desperately pressured her to have an abortion, who never gave her a dime or a helping hand as she struggled, a stranger in a foreign land with almost no money, to take care of a baby, and who has never helped her since. He is the man who didn't want her and, worse, didn't want the greatest treasure she could offer—Michael—either. What's too painful? It just hurts Bonnie too much to see how much her only son loves the man who hurt her so.

In a good-enough marriage, the mother helps the child idealize the father. She, like the child, has every interest in exaggerating his good points and minimizing his flaws. When family members go their separate ways, withdraw from the family as a unit, either through divorce or failure to marry, this is no longer true either emotionally or economically. A husband sees his child and his own economic interests as one. He works for the family. A father who is no longer part of his son's household, however, experiences supporting his son as a drain on his own household and often on his ability to attract a new wife and support a new family. He particularly objects to the fact that his child support money unavoidably will help his ex-wife or girlfriend as well as his kids. Full of ambivalence, the good man pays anyway and a bad man absconds. But either way, he and his children experience the hard, inescapable reality: When marriage ends, the financial and erotic interests of family members fundamentally diverge.

Fathers, in turn, complain about the awkwardness and artificiality of the postdivorce relationship with their children, about the demotion from head of the household to visiting daddy.

"Few people realize how difficult it is to transplant the relationship from the rich soil of family life to the impoverished ground of the visiting relationship."[16] One of the sad and surprising truths we are beginning to face is that unmarriage radically alters the father-child relationship. The children almost always experience this transformation as a profound loss.

Once again, it depends on your point of view. From the fathers' standpoint, many are just doing the best they can in a difficult situation. Maybe they didn't want the divorce anyway (the majority of divorces are initiated by women[17]); maybe they desperately wanted to be real fathers in real families and instead are thrust into this fractured half-a-dad position, each visit a reminder that they aren't a real father but a visiting one. Maybe the kids are hostile, too, or acting weird, because of the divorce or because of their mother's hostility—who knows? The dad usually doesn't. The financial squeeze is tight, and he resents helping to support a woman who wants his money but doesn't want him. If having a father was so important for the kids, why couldn't she stick around and stay married, as she'd promised?

Under these circumstances, the man who stays in touch and pays his child support regularly is likely to feel quite good about his performance as a father.

The postdivorce fathers in Wallerstein's study were an unusually committed group compared to national averages. Very few fathers had abandoned their children completely. Ten years after the divorce, only 10 percent of children saw their fathers once a year or less. This greater paternal involvement is consistent with studies that show educated men are most likely to keep in contact with their kids after divorce.[18] Wallerstein's children were all drawn from middle-class families in which the fathers were mostly college-educated professionals.

These fathers, generally remarried, in demanding professions, and living busy, complicated lives, made special efforts to keep in touch with their kids. For the most part, they paid their court-ordered child support. From their point of view, they have done well in a difficult situation, certainly much better than the average guy.

Yet the children feel and experience the same situation entirely differently. "Most fathers in our study thought they had done reasonably well in fulfilling their obligations whereas three out of four of the children felt rejected by their fathers. . . ." The father says, "My door is always open. My son is welcome to come visit me anytime, and I'll give him anything he needs." The son says, "I'm not welcome in his house. I feel awkward and uncomfortable there. All I do is watch television while he talks to his friends."[19]

What mattered to children, in Wallerstein's experience, was not the amount of time but the quality of the relationship. Boys who saw their fathers as moral and competent, and who felt valued by them, did very well. When fathers were seen as bad, weak, or unconcerned, boys were likely to suffer "low self-esteem, poor grades, weak aspirations."[20]

But mothers who have been abandoned by or who have left their children's father generally are not very able to assist children to see the father as good, strong, and concerned. If the father has abandoned the family, it is hard for the mother to see him as loving and concerned. Otherwise, if he is so good, strong, and concerned, how can she justify to the children her decision to leave?

In divorce, both children and father feel the loss of the connecting link: the loss of the mother's love for the father. For, to a considerable and unrecognized extent, the father's role is sustained through and by women. When women (many for very understandable reasons) refuse to take on this burden, the one who suffers is their child.

These underlying erotic truths explain one of the great puzzles in the sociological literature: the vast difference that exists between children of divorce and children whose fathers die.

Children have very different psychological reactions to parental death and parental divorce. Children who are orphaned react by internalizing. They frequently withdraw for a time, in grief, to mourn. By contrast, children of divorce, especially boys, are far more likely to externalize, to act out and develop behavior problems. Similarly, girls who lose a father to death often become shy and reserved with members of the opposite sex, while girls in divorced families often respond by launching into precocious, sexualized relations with males. Children of divorce are also far more likely to end up divorced as adults compared to children who lose a parent to death.

Of the two ways to lose a father, death is better. As sociologist Robert Emery, surveying the evidence, concludes, "Compared to children from homes disrupted by death, children from divorced homes have more psychological problems."[21]

This finding is, in some ways, surprising. From the way sociologists conceptualize the family—as a set of tasks and roles—there is little difference between the loss of a father to death or through divorce. Both represent cases of "paternal absence"; in both cases, mothers must take up the slack left by the loss of their partner, a daunting task that may lead to role overload. Some have gone so far as to argue that something called "family breakup" is really not much more common today than it was a hundred years ago, when divorce rates were low and illegitimacy almost nonexistent, but many more children were orphaned.

In theory, it makes no sense, but the data show that it is nonetheless true: Losing a parent to death is not at all like losing a father through divorce. Orphans and divorce orphans are going through two different experiences, and of the two, divorce is far more traumatic.

Children often may experience their parent's death as a form of abandonment—but at some deep level they know, or come to understand, that this is not true. Death, unlike divorce, is not a failure of love. Their parents did not choose to leave them. Moreover, in death, unlike divorce, the mother who remains still loves and admires their father. She usually even idealizes him far more in death than in life. They may lose their father's flesh-and-blood presence, but the story of their father—of the man who made them, loved them, protected them—remains intact.

The same disturbing truth emerges from another set of social science research. In the aftermath of the divorce revolution, experts put much emphasis on the need for both parents to keep close ties to their kids after a divorce. But surprisingly, evidence is mounting that frequent visiting is no balm for father hunger. Even when fathers stay, children may feel abandoned. Children of divorce who see their fathers do, on average, no better than children of divorce who do not.

Wallerstein found to her surprise that "the sense of loss the children experience is unrelated to how often they are visited." Even the 10 percent of children who, ten years after the divorce, still saw their fathers once or twice a week feel rejected by him.[22] Wallerstein's study is based on a small, middle-class sample. But large-scale studies seem to confirm this result.

In the NSC (National Survey of Children) study, for example, the amount of contact children had with absent fathers made little difference in their well-being. As scholars Frank Furstenberg and Andrew Cherlin note, "Teenagers who saw their fathers regularly were just as likely as those with infrequent contact to have problems in school or engage in delinquent acts and precocious sexual behavior."[23] Nor was kids' conduct related to the amount of intimacy and identification they had with their noncustodial fathers. When these same kids were reinterviewed in 1987, when they were ages eighteen to twenty-three, those who had close ties to their fathers were no more successful than those who did not. To their surprise, researchers have found that the father inside of marriage and the father outside of marriage are just not the same thing.

Here is the puzzle the current research poses: Although the presence of an active father makes a great difference in children's well-being inside of marriage, the presence of that same father outside of marriage seems not to have anything like the same benefits for children.

And it is the father's role that appears particularly fragile and vulnerable to disruption. For example, noncustodial mothers are more likely than fathers to keep in regular touch with their kids. Children who do not live with their mothers are almost as likely as other children to report they have a good relationship with their mother (60 versus 57 percent). But when fathers move out of the home, the relationship deteriorates rapidly: 69 percent of children who live with their fathers report a good relationship, but only 36 percent of children with absent fathers enjoy a good relationship with him.[24]

More than half of children whose fathers don't live with them say they don't get all the affection they need from their fathers. Those who saw their absent fathers frequently did not evaluate their relationships more favorably than those who saw them infrequently. (Worst were those who did not see their fathers at all.) Only half of absent fathers were viewed as "family" by their children compared to all fathers living with their children and even 70 percent of stepfathers.

After years of exclusive focus on the mother-child bond, experts are rediscovering the importance of fathers. Indeed, as Judith Wallerstein remarked, "[I]t is the children of divorce who taught us very early that to be separated from their father was intolerable. The poignancy of their reactions is astounding, especially among the six-, seven-, and eight-year-olds. They cry for their daddies—be they good, bad or indifferent daddies. I have been deeply struck by the distress children of every age suffer at losing their fathers."[25]

In response to studies like these, psychologists and other child care experts began to emphasize the importance of fathering, and to urge us to find new ways to involve fathers in children's lives outside of marriage. Joint custody swept the land, new rhetorical attacks on deadbeat dads were launched, and parenting groups for unwed fathers began to spring up.

Programs like these reflect a new hope: Perhaps, if we can transform divorced husbands and never-married men into dependable fathers, we can undo the damage of divorce before it happens. Divorce (and failure to marry) could be remade into a kinder, gentler institution. "People are only starting to recognize the importance of including teen fathers," says Beth Grube, dean of social work at Fordham University's Tarrytown campus, which is starting a new program for young unwed fathers. "It's not only good for the father, but for the mother and child."[26]

As part of this new spirit of optimism, the Clinton administration proposed $390 billion for job training, parent education, and counseling programs for unwed fathers.[27] But the peculiar problems unwed fathers face are not easy to overcome. Consider the case of Hassam Lemons. Hassam was a seventeen-year-old unmarried father of a baby girl when he entered a program run by the National Institute for Responsible Fatherhood, a Chicago-based group that motivates young unwed fathers to take responsibility for their kids. When he and his girlfriend split up, Hassam dropped out of his daughter's life.

"The people from the institute kept saying 'Where's your child? That's really taking it out on her.'" So Hassam made contact again, and now that he has found work as a handyman, he says he'll pay child support. There is one complication, however. He recently fathered another child, and now he says he needs to spend more time (and presumably money) with his new girl and his new baby.

Hassam means well. But outside of marriage, he finds it almost impossible to be a committed father. Marriage unifies the erotic interests of the family. In marriage, a man and a woman give themselves to each other in a sexual union that includes a promise to care for each other and for any children that result. Released from marriage, the erotic interests of individuals necessarily fragment as the family diversifies.

What does it mean to be a good father? At a basic level, a father shows his children and their mother that he loves them by putting their needs first. His sexuality is (in theory) at his wife's disposal, not other women's—and cannot therefore threaten the well-being of his children. His income is their income. His emotional and financial energy is also theirs. In the act of marriage, a man makes a supreme commitment to protect and care for his family.

But what if there are two children and two mothers to care for? His commitment to both cannot be supreme. The result is that, even for men who wish to be responsible fathers, often one set of children must, for all practical purposes, be subordinated to another.

Several studies confirm that for fathers, "remarriage frequently introduce[s] new parental obligations . . . weakening his ties with his biological offspring. In effect, sociological parenthood took precedence over biological parenthood."[28] Nor are the erotic dilemmas all of the fathers' own making. Ricky Hall, for example, is a twenty-five-year-old currently enrolled in Beat the Streets, a Cleveland job-training program for unwed fathers. Ricky promises he'll pay child support as soon as he finds a job, and says he wants to visit his kids right now. But his former girlfriend has acquired a new boyfriend—and he's jealous. "I could go and start trouble, but I choose not to," Ricky says.[29]

The mother's erotic interests also diversify outside of marriage. Her new partner may or may not be interested in her kids, and he may or may not be tolerant of her ex-lover. Outside of marriage, her love for her children and for her lover may well be at odds. And, of course, when marriage fails to unify a family, a mother's love for her kids may be at war with her hatred for their father.

Despite the fact that the children seldom saw their fathers, they did not forget them. In the postmarital family, a startling gap arises between mother's perceptions and children's perceptions over who counts as a family member. In one large-scale study, half of the children who did not live with their fathers nonetheless named their fathers as members of their family, while only one in twenty of their mothers did so.[30]

When, as is often the case in families fractured by divorce or a failure to marry, the father is a man of very limited resources, struggling to get by in a world where the wages of less educated men are falling precipitately, the difficulties of being a good dad to two or more sets of children intensify. But for all fathers, time, energy, and money are limited commodities. In difficult circumstances, some men choose to abandon their kids. Others simply are forced to prioritize. The children demoted to the second best know it and suffer for it.

David's mother and father divorced several years ago. She moved back to New York to be closer to family. Every summer David goes to visit his dad and returns heartbroken. "David's so hungry for his father, but his dad never spends time with him," his mom complains. "He always has to tag along with his father's new wife's daughters."

But as David's dad points out, what else can you expect? "These kids are my family," he says, not unreasonably, from an adult point of view. But nevertheless, as a result, David will never experience himself as his father's first priority. For the few weeks David gets to see his dad, David will always have to split his father's care and attention not (as most children do) with his brothers and sisters but with a couple of complete strangers. To David, it doesn't seem fair. To David's father, it seems the best he can possibly be expected to do.

Nor did joint custody live up to its billing—a way to retain the unity of parenting, a father and a mother, equally devoted to their children, after marriage fractures. According to Furstenberg and Cherlin's review of the literature, "Joint legal custody seems to be hardly distinguishable in practice from maternal sole custody."[31] The evidence for the effect of joint physical custody is less established (as the number of such families is quite small), but at least two studies also suggest that children in joint physical custody "were no better adjusted than children from the mother-physical custody families".[32] Children in these families may see their fathers more, but their parents may also quarrel more as a result.[33] What is important is not just the physical presence of the father but the moral unity of the parents. When Eros fractures, the child is torn between irreconcilable differences. Subsumed by a longing to incorporate both parents into his or her very self, the child instead experiences intense loyalty conflicts, beholden to two parents who no longer love or are loyal to each other.

Young teens whose parents were divorced are almost four times as likely to say they experience "family-related moral dilemmas" than children of intact families. Moreover, children of divorce face very different kinds of moral conflict than children in intact families: "The early adolescents of divorce were concerned with deciding which parent to live with and not hurting their feelings, whereas the early adolescents from intact families were concerned with fighting with siblings." At the same time, children of divorce also were more likely to express problems with peers and friends (35 percent versus 9 percent).[34]

Marriage is the vehicle by which, throughout history, society creates ties between men and their children. The current fumbling that attempts to reproduce these ties outside of marriage is without precedent and unlikely to succeed for the simple reason that marriage and parenting are not, as the experts have imagined, job labels that can be transferred from one employee to the next as personnel shift, but something else entirely: erotic relations.

The separation of "the sexual alliance" from "the parenting alliance" is not, as family utopians such as Drucilla Cornell seem to imagine, a new idea, but was in fact the basis of countless nineteenth century utopian communities (not to mention quite a number of 1960s communes) none of which survived.

Moreover, the separation of the sexual alliance from the parenting alliance already is being tried on a mass scale in this country: It's called divorce. We don't have to argue about the effectiveness of this strategy in theory; the results are empirically available: For men, the sexual alliance takes precedence over the parental alliance. For women, the separation of parental and romantic love creates tensions and conflicts within the household that are not easy to reconcile.

The last thirty years have taught us that it is far easier to break down an old norm than to build up a new one; easier to tell men and women they don't have to stay married than to faithfully fulfill the visionary's alternate conception of their family duty.

The flight from fatherhood is generated in large part by an unwillingness to recognize that choices have costs, not all of them paid by the one who chooses. Family visionaries like Cornell paint a scenario in which the relationships adults choose will almost by definition be in the best interests of their children (what makes me happy makes my family better off), regardless of the substance of what is chosen.

Isn't it feminism that first taught us to escape from this myth of family unity—that the interests of wives and husbands, parents and children, are always and everywhere the same? Yet we see here, under the guise of "diversity," a resurrection of this same myth: that human interests never conflict, that we always can follow our desires at no cost to our children's hearts.

Marriage plays a crucial role in attaching men in particular to children. Marriage creates a unity of interest between them and their children and a distinctly male role in the family. When marriage dissolves or is ignored, this crucial tie between men and children apparently is not just weakened, it is transformed in ways that are hostile to the interests of children—to their profound desire for union with their parents. It is not biology, but law, custom, and mores that make fathers out of men. But, as we are discovering, the fact that the tie between father and child is less "natural," that is, more fragile, more a product of culture, than that binding mother and child does not mean that it is less important. Culture is, after all, man's natural state, our inescapable destiny. But it does mean that attaching men to their children, creating a tie so firm a child's heart can rely on it, is a social problem, in the way that creating attachment between women and their children is not.

How do we give children the fathers they need and long for? Marriage is the ancient answer to that ancient problem, and none of the modern solutions that attempt to re-create the father outside of marriage or make unrelated adults do a father's work appear likely to assuage our children's hunger.

NOTES

1. Judith Wallerstein, speech given before the Second Annual Congress of American Family and Conciliation Courts, June 6, 1997.
2. Ibid.
3. Ibid.
4. Barbara Dafoe Whitehead, *The Divorce Culture* (New York: Knopf, 1997).
5. Arlene S. Skolnick and Jerome H. Skolnick, *Family in Transition,* 5th ed. (Boston: Little, Brown and Company, 1986), 371-372.
6. Dr. Morton H. Shaevetz and Marjories Hansen Shaevitz, "How Men Really Feel," *The Superwoman Syndrome* (New York: Warner Books, 1984), 55-56.
7. Nina J. Eaton, "Life Without Father," *Los Angeles Times Magazine,* June 14, 1992, 18.
8. Frank F. Furstenberg, Jr., Christine Winquist Nord, James L. Peterson, and Nicholas Zill, "The Life Course of Children of Divorce: Marital Disruption and Parental Contact," *American Sociological Review,* 48 no. 5 (October 1995), 663.
9. Frank F. Furstenberg, Jr., and Andrew J. Cherlin, *Divided Families: What Happens to Children When Parents Part* (Cambridge, MA: Harvard University Press, 1991), 35-36.
10. Furstenberg et al, "The Life Course of Children of Divorce," 667.

11. Roger A. Wojtkiewicz, "Diversity in Experiences of Parental Structure During Childhood and Adolescence," *Demography* 29, no. 1 (February 1992): 59-67.

12. Susan Chira, "Novel Idea in Welfare Planning: Helping Children by Helping Their Fathers," *New York Times* March 30, 1994, B6. See also *Young Unwed Fathers: Changing Roles and Emerging Policies,* Robert I. Lerman and Theodora J. Ooms (eds.) (Philadelphia: Temple University Press, 1993).

13. Furstenberg, "The Life Course of Children of Divorce," 663.

14. "The Mainstreaming of Single Motherhood," *San Francisco Chronicle,* July 20, 1993, C3.

15. Judith S. Wallerstein and Sandra Blakeslee, *Second Chances: Men, Women, and Children a Decade After Divorce* (New York: Ticknor and Fields, 1989), 234.

16. Ibid., 235.

17. See, for example, Furstenberg and Cherline, *Divided Families,* 22.

18. See, for example, Nicholas Zill and Carolyn Rogers, "Recent Trends in the Well-Being of Children in the United States and Their Implications for Public Policy," in John L. Palmer and Isabel V. Sawhill (eds.), *The Changing American Family and Public Policy* (Washington, DC: The Urban Institute Press, 1988), 44.

19. Wallerstein and Blakeslee, *Second Chances,* 238.

20. Ibid.

21. Robert E. Emery, *Marriage, Divorce, and Children's Adjustment* (Newbury Park, CA: Sage Publications, 1988), 94. For Emery's summary of the literature comparing divorce and death, see pp. 57 and 67.

22. Wallerstein speech, 1997.

23. Furstenberg and Cherlin, *Divided Families.*

24. James L. Peterson and Nicholas Zill, "Marital Disruption, Parent-Child Relationships, and Behavior Problems in Children," *Journal of Marriage and the Family* 48, no. 2 (May 1986): 295-307.

25. Wallerstein speech, 1997.

26. Chira, "Novel Idea in Welfare Planning," *New York Times,* March 30, 1994, 6.

27. Ibid.

28. Furstenberg, et al., "The Life Course of Children of Divorce," 666.

29. Chira, "Novel Idea in Welfare Planning," B6.

30. Frank F. Furstenberg and Christine Winquist Nord, "Parenting Apart: Patterns of Child-Rearing After Marital Disruption," *Journal of Marriage and the Family* 47 (November, 1985), 889.

31. Furstenberg and Cherlin, *Divided Families,* 74.

32. Ibid., 74-75.

33. The literature documenting the negative effects of parental conflict is now large and well-established. For a good summary, see Emery, *Marriage, Divorce and Children's Adjustment,* 94-95.

34. Dorothy Tysse Breen and Margaret Crosbie-Burnett, "Moral Dilemmas of Early Adolescents of Divorced and Intact Families: A Qualitative and Quantitative Analysis," *Journal of Early Adolescence* 13, no. 2 (May 1993): 168-182.

NINE

FATHERHOOD AND ITS DISCONTENTS:
MEN, PATRIARCHY, AND FREEDOM

Drucilla Cornell

THE PROGRAM OF THE FATHER'S MOVEMENT:
"THE CARROT AT THE END OF THE STICK"

The Stick

THERE IS A GROWING MOVEMENT in the United States made up
primarily of heterosexual White men—joined by some White
women—who hail the promised return of responsible husbands
who will end the toil and trouble of single mothers.

According to the movement, there are two main impediments
to men becoming *father* again. The first impediment is the nature
of man. Few women, even in their worst fantasies and fears about
what men are really like, view men as bleakly as does David
Blankenhorn, author of *Fatherless America: Confronting Our Most
Urgent Social Problem.*[1] For Blankenhorn, whose description of
men is echoed throughout the father's movement, men are by
nature irresponsible, slovenly, murderously aggressive, rapacious,
and polygamous, if one even can dignify their need to spew their

sperm as widely as possible by identifying it with an institutional structure. Such ribald creatures, if left to themselves, will desert their families, inevitably yielding to their licentious sexuality and their socially disruptive impulses. So, of course, they cannot be left to themselves if we are to solve the problem of fatherlessness and all the social ills that result from this pernicious reality. Stern measures must be taken against men both directly and indirectly so that they are forced to curb the urges that they cannot control otherwise.

But there is reason to be optimistic as long as we as a people lay down the law and conscript (Blankenhorn's word) men into fatherhood and monogamy. The historical analysis offered by the movement portrays a past in which social forces such as religion played a much greater role in reining men in than they do now. Men have been effectively forced into the role of father before, and they can be again. But we will need to change our licentious cultural environment that does nothing to impede men from giving in to their nature. According to the movement, we have to press earnestly for laws that either prohibit or at least limit access to divorce. We will have to take action, both legal and otherwise, to track down deadbeat dads and bring them back home. Once we have rounded them up, we also will need to educate men about the role of the good family man. Most of the responsibility for men's education is to fall on women. Crucial to the success of actually keeping men in place once they are conscripted into family life is the feeling that women need them. According to movement organizers, women have unfortunately gotten used to men being out of the picture, and, indeed, some even seem inclined to continue life without father. Thus, this movement contends that we must close the sperm banks so that women will have to have a "real" man to get pregnant. But since men are to be needed as fathers and not just as sperm donors, this is only the first step in bringing men back into the fold. Men have to be needed as breadwinners just as we remember them from the popular family television shows of the 1950s. Crucial to the program, then, is the end to Aid to Families with Dependent Children (AFDC), because welfare makes single motherhood possible and therefore encourages male irresponsibility. The fathers' movement is convinced that if we are vigilant and take the necessary measures to circumscribe alternatives to the 1950s television model of the nuclear family, we will get men to comply with the role of the good family man. After all, we have had success in conscripting men into war, even though, as literature and historical memoirs teach us, men's nature was as often as not to run away from rather than into the line of fire.

The Carrot

But the fathers' movement does not just want to use the stick against men, it also wants to dangle the carrot to entice them. Something about the role of the good family man has to be attractive if men are to take it on with the enthusiasm and energy it demands. Here again is where women come in. Women need to make men feel big in their role. The father is not to be just another parent immersed in all the nitty-gritty day-to-day tasks of parenting. He is to be the *father* with all the authority and power that that word supposedly inspires. His is the man's role, and other members of the family are to recognize that only a real man can play it well. According to the fathers' movement, rigid gender division in the family is necessary to make the father's role manly and dominant enough for men to want to play it.[2]

Long Live the King

It is the insistence on rigid gender division within the family that pits the fathers' movement against feminists. After all, one whole school of feminism in psychology seems to be as vehement in its insistence on the importance of men playing a parenting role to the creation of a happy family life and to the development of the well-being of its members as is the fathers' movement.[3] Of course, the goal of object relations or relational[4] psychology is to analyze the psychoanalytic source of the separation of masculinity from the care and intimacy associated with parenting. Object relations theory does not accept the premise of the fathers' movement that men are by nature rakish creatures who must be ruthlessly trained. The analysis provided by object relations theory finds the source of the split of masculinity from qualities associated with mothering in the perpetuation of rigidly defined gender roles within the family.

Object relations analysts provide clinical support in defense of a diversity of masculinities and femininities that belie the claims of the fathers' movement about men's nature. This already-lived diversity shows the promise of a variety of families, homosexual and heterosexual, and the possibility of a masculinity that does not define itself against the qualities needed to be a loving parent. The divergence with the fathers' movement is precisely over what maketh a father and not over the desirability of men playing a much more active role in child care whether they are members of a heterosexual nuclear family or not. The fathers' movement attacks all feminists because they purportedly want to rid families of men and encourage women to take their children and run. This is simply not the case.

Most of us who are mothers want all the help we can get, and we will take it when it's offered. Of course, we also don't want to lose the right to our children because we seek that help yet refuse to live our lives in accordance with the fantasy of "the good mother."[5] We need to make a distinction that will help us understand exactly why the fathers' movement is so hostile to feminists. The movement is not out to encourage men to parent. Indeed, members are hostile to the extended kinship systems many of us are creating that do involve men in much more active parenting roles than those given to men in the 1950s television programs so cherished in the movement. By "a good family man," they do not mean that the man gets up in the middle of the night just as often as the woman does; they don't mean that he changes as many diapers or even comes close to it; they certainly don't mean that he takes his daughter to ballet class while his partner works.

Simply put, the fathers' movement does not want men to parent—they want them to *father,* and they have very specific ideas about what fathering entails. First and foremost, it means the persistent reinforcement of the rigid gender divide in the family so that men can rest assured that they will not be "femmed" by their acceptance of the role of the good family man. Indeed, the carrot to entice men back to the family is the promise that, as *father,* men can be little kings in their own domain. Feminists are clearly the enemies of this movement since, despite our differences, we all join in the refrain that the emperor has no clothes. And for good reason. Women have endured horrible suffering in the "castles" of men who have been legally allowed to indulge their fantasies of what it means to rule their families without threat of outside invasion.

THE SUBJECTION OF MEN AND THE FEMINIST CRITIQUE OF PATRIARCHY

Two Stories

Since the fathers' movement has focused almost exclusively on men, it is not surprising that its organizers have paid no attention to the feminist analysis of the link between male violence and the carrot offered by the movement that each man as a father can be king in his own "castle." But it also has not given attention to the toll masculinity as imagined by the fathers' movement takes on men. According to the fathers' movement, men desert their families because it is their nature to do so. Without the cultural framework of coercion and encouragement advocated in the movement's program, there will be further erosion of the family structure. The movement's solution is to rebuild the family in the style of those showcased in the 1950s when both men and women knew their proper places. But is the problem correctly identified solely as a cultural one?

The answer is no. To justify my answer, I want to present the feminist critique of masculinity and of patriarchy as it analyzes the trap these set for men. To make this critique come alive, I will tell the story of two male auto workers who both ultimately left their families. Unfortunately, my stories are true (names are pseudonyms).[6]

Jim Nelson was fifty-three years old when he was laid off from his job. Nelson had been a skilled electrician in a Michigan auto plant for some twenty-five years. He was laid off in 1995. That year he had earned $52,000, which included the overtime that he often took. He had children ranging from thirteen to twenty-seven. He had put his two oldest children through college. His wife had stayed home when the children were young. To help out with college expenses, she had taken a part-time job as a secretary, which she held at the time Nelson was laid off. Nelson, who had always worked long hours and had taken pride in his work, felt completely lost after he became unemployed. His union benefits supplemented his unemployment check so that with the help of his wife's earnings, they could still make ends meet. His wife took on full-time work to help out. The fact that his wife was the one who went out to work now and he had to take over "female" household responsibilities humiliated him. He confided in friends that he no longer felt like a man. For months after he was laid off, he vigilantly looked for work that was close to the level of skill and pay of his position as an electrician. He had no success. Finally, in defeat, he began to look for much less skilled jobs with considerably less pay. He still had no luck. He was always given some reason why he was not right for the job: He was too old and/or overqualified. Finally, he gave up. He began spending his days in bars. Often when he was drunk, he physically abused his wife. The couple went into counseling, but Nelson was in such deep despair over what he saw as his failure to fulfill his role as a man that he could not be helped.

After twenty-nine years of marriage, his wife felt she had no other choice but to leave him. One year to the day after he was laid off, he turned the gun he used for hunting against himself.

Nelson's tragic story gives a human face to the economic reality reported in *The State of Working America* published by the Economic Policy Institute.[7] Workers making over $50,000 counted for twice the percentage of lost jobs at the end of the 1980s than they did at the end of 1970s. Three million workers in 1995 were affected by layoffs, a figure that is 50 percent higher than the number of people affected by violent crime. Since 1979, forty-nine million jobs in the higher-skilled range, such as the one Nelson held, have been lost to the economy. In one-third of all the households in the United States, one family member has lost a job in the last five years. One in ten adults reports that the loss of a job has caused both a financial and a personal crisis leading to estrangement or divorce.

My second story is that of Sam Morris. Morris was a friend of Nelson's. They worked at the same plant for almost the same number of years. Due to affirmative action, Morris, an African American, was allowed to train as an electrician in 1972. He also was laid off in 1995. Morris made $48,000 the year he was laid off. Like Nelson, Morris was determined at first to find a comparable job. Morris admitted to becoming increasingly depressed as the months dragged on without any hope of skilled employment. His wife had worked for over ten years as a waitress at a local restaurant. Like many African American couples, she worked nights while he worked days because they could not afford adequate after-school care. Morris joked that maybe being forced to see each other led to their separation. About one year after Morris had lost his job, he moved out. He began to seek jobs at every possible level of skill and pay. When his sixteen-year-old son who worked at McDonald's gave him the tip that there might be jobs opening up there, he went immediately to get an application. In a recent study, Katharine Newman and Carol Stack show that for every job at McDonald's, there are fourteen applicants.[8] Morris was not one of the lucky ones. He did not get hired at McDonald's. He recently found and took a job as a part-time bus boy.

For both Nelson and Morris work was not only, or even primarily, about money. The capacity to be the breadwinner in the family was deeply tied in with the sense of their worth as men. Morris' position in particular had provided him with security that most African Americans can still not hope to aspire to because of continuing discrimination. After his layoff, Morris was diagnosed with hypertension. A recent study has shown that hypertension among African Americans is the leading cause of heart attacks.[9] The study further traced a connection between hypertension and economic insecurity. This economic insecurity is part of the reality of continuing discrimination, as Black workers continue to have twice the unemployment rate of Whites.

Parenting and Economic Hope

Both Morris and Nelson, prior to his suicide, could no longer maintain their marriages. Both were men who had prided themselves on being good family men. They had both had long marriages. They both were the primary breadwinners in the family. They both identified the primary role of the father as that of the breadwinner. A major change in their economic capacity to support their families affected them deeply in their lives as husbands and fathers. Yet the fathers' movement has ignored completely the impact of the downsizing of the workforce in the United States on men in their family lives.

Studies have shown that both men and women connect their capacity to parent with economic security. More specifically, parenting introduces the need for economic planning and thus, of course, of an economic future. The most obvious example for those who can afford it is "saving for college." But children demand the ability to anticipate a stable economic future in innumerable day-to-day ways. Medical costs have to be covered. Dental costs are also an enormous expense. An ability to know that the costs of maintaining a child can be met even if one loses a job demands financial planning and savings needed to plan with. The downsizing of America has wreaked havoc with people's economic expectations. More and more young people express concern that they will not be able to afford children.

The stories of Nelson and Morris represent the worst nightmares of many workers. There were simply no jobs at their skill or compensation level. Work was so much a part of their identity that they both desperately wanted to find another job. Morris jumped at the job of a busboy. The centrality of work to men's lives has long been documented.[10] The fathers' movement completely fails to grasp how its own vision of what makes a man a man can play a role in the terrible tragedy of Jim Nelson's life. Nelson certainly wasn't an irresponsible drifter. He wasn't a womanizer. Outlawing divorce, closing sperm banks, and cutting single mothers off welfare certainly would not have helped him.

Crucial to his sense of well-being would have been the ability to find a job that would use his skills and allow him to feel like a productive member of society as well the breadwinner to his family. Any program that took families seriously, including one like the fathers' movement that purportedly wants to make men responsible parents, would have to address the economic realities that are undermining family life. Job retraining, an increase in the minimum wage (a bill that recently passed Congress), and health insurance should all be viewed as central to any encompassing program to value families. Clearly neither Morris nor Nelson needed the stick to be a "good family man."

There's No Such Thing as *Father* and It's a Good Thing, Too[11]

But did the so-called carrot of paternal authority in which the man is established as the little king of his family deliver on its promise? Isn't gender hierarchy with its rigid roles and identities implicated in Nelson's death and Morris's despair? Nelson's unemployment brought on an identity crisis that was so pervasive that he ended his life. Does the analysis of men offered to us by the fathers' movement help us in any way to understand the depths of these men's despair, especially because their supplementary benefits kept them from having to face immediate financial devastation? The fathers' movement argues that men need at least an illusion of power over women and children because only then will they rein in their aggression and sexual licentiousness. This so-called argument relies on an appeal to men's nature. But the appeal to men's nature doesn't explain the despair and the sense of worthlessness both Morris and Nelson experienced. After all, they could have used their free time screeching around on motorcycles and getting laid every afternoon. Instead they desperately looked for work, day in and day out.

Psychoanalysis, and here I am relying primarily on Jacques Lacan's[12] reading of Freud's account of the Oedipal complex, can help us understand the despair of these men. Following Freud, Lacan argues that what we think of as our civilized life, our culture, is inseparable from patriarchy, the transmission of family identity through the name of the Father. Lacanian theory, like most schools of psychoanalytic theory, posits the link between mother and child as a dyadic relation formed in the intimate bond of pregnancy and, later, of breastfeeding. The fathers' movement shares this naturalized understanding of the mother/child relationship, which is why it is assumed as unproblematic. Women, movement advocates assume, will be responsible mothers unless unduly influenced by feminists to go against their natures. Feminists have challenged this naturalization of the mother/child relationship.[13]

For our purposes here, we need to understand how patriarchal family organization, with its set qualities for what makes a father, imposes a toll on men. In Lacanian theory, human beings enter culture and acquire the ability to become speaking beings only after they experience a radical cut from unitary bliss with the maternal body. For Lacan, infants are driven into language by their registration that the mother is not there just for him or her. The initial fantasy of the infant is that, in their dyadic unity, the infant and the mother are one. Where she goes, so goes the infant. Her breast is the child's. But, of course, this fantasy cannot last; the mother is a separate person. She has her own life. She leaves. The infant has to call out to her, literally scream for her to bring her back into the room. That Mommy can and does leave causes great anxiety in the infant. The infant begins to resist this traitor for robbing this imagined total security. Of course, this kind of absolute security is a fantasy. The condition of this fantasy is that the mother cannot be a sexual being with her own desires. The fantasy figure on whom the infant is totally dependent is the Phallic Mother. She contains everything in herself and, therefore, her own need will not drive her away from the infant. Once the fantasized mother/child dyad is shattered, the Phallic Mother "remains" in the imaginary as all-powerful and threatening in her power both to bestow and take away life. She returns in cartoons. Like the Sea Witch in Disney's *The Little Mermaid,* this scary Phallic Mother is unconsciously contrasted with the actual Mother who is now found to be incomplete, a being split in affections by desire. The "scar of the navel" is not only actual in birth, it is also a symbolic tear that rips us away from the imagined cocoon of the preoedipal phase.

The introduction of the child into the "rules" of adulthood, what Lacan calls the symbolic order, is at the expense of the Mother/Other and all that she represents. The law that imposes this symbolic castration is symbolized in the actual institutional structures and laws of patriarchal culture. The signifier for this law is the phallus, which we know only as the law that bars us from the mother. We know this law in mythology for the dire effects imposed upon anyone who breaks it. But, in Lacan, breaking the law is no longer the literal incest taboo, it becomes the more sweeping metaphor of resisting patriarchal order. This explains why, for Lacan, the ultimate cultural law is the law imposed by the

Oedipus complex. Both sexes are barred by the law imposed by the name of the father from the return to the fantasized mother/child dyad and all it comes to represent in patriarchal culture.

The anxiety generated by the loss of the mother/child dyad turns the child toward the father because in the oedipal crisis, he is the one who is recognized as the object of the mother's desire. But what is it that singles out the father? In other words, what is it that Daddy has that Mommy desires? The simple answer is the penis but Lacanians would never put it so simply. The identification with the father is inseparable from the projection of the power to control the mother, to literally give her a name and in that sense to guarantee that she and correspondingly, the infant, are spoken for.

Thus, it is the name of the father, his representation as the source of blood ties, that is the basis for identification with him and not the simple fact that he has a penis. The biological penis takes on significance for the little boy because it is identified with the power to assume a place in society. This power is established by patrilineage, which identifies the father's line as the one that constitutes the family. It is only very recently that children not given their father's name but recognized as his blood have not been ostracized as "bastards" and rendered social outcasts. Some current Republican politicians would have us return to those days.

On this account, the penis is identified with the phallus as the symbol of potency and the representation of family continuity because of the infant's idealization of the actual father. If the penis were not read through the context of patriarchy and the legal power it gives to the father, a penis would be just a penis. The little boy can identify himself through his projection of his likeness to the father who has the penis. It is this unconscious identification of the phallus with the penis that allows the little boy, at least on the level of fantasy, to compensate for the fundamental loss of the dream of bliss he has to endure to enter civilized order. Psychically, those who become men have their subjectivity organized around this fantasy and accept the tolls of civilization precisely because of the compensation it offers for a primary loss, an imaginary world where discontentment would no longer be the price we pay for becoming human.

The "bad news" for the little boy is that the fantasy leaves him in a constant state of anxiety before the terror that what makes him a man can always be taken away from him by the imaginary father with whom he unconsciously identifies. The endless substitutions for this father, in the form of deans, chief executive officers, politicians, and other figures of powerful men leave him in unconsciously accepted subordination. His masculinity is always on the line, and thus we have an explanation of the gesture mandated by the pecking order among men: "Just don't take it away from me and I'll work sixteen hours a day and never talk back." This is hardly an account of actual male superiority, yet it is an account of why men need the fantasy that they are superior to women.

The cultural analysis of the fathers' movement echoes the need for men to be offered power over women in order to accept their actual roles in society, roles that more often than not are a far cry from the idealized father of infancy. The fathers' movement is also right that feminists are the ultimate resisters of the law of patriarchy. Feminists have been fighting for centuries for the political realization that women are persons, a battle that at least for this feminist demands that we define personhood away from its containment by unconscious associations of the human as man. Yet man himself is imprisoned by the very masculinity that purportedly gives him his status as man. On the Lacanian account of masculinity I have just offered, there is clearly a basis for an alliance to challenge the structures of gender. The attributes of masculinity are fixed by the identification with the idealized father. A man who fails to measure up, and he eventually will since the ideal father is not real, loses his very sense of self.

Under this ideal of masculinity, loss of a job can be understood as a terrible failure to measure up. The carrot of masculine power is inseparable from the freezing of gender traits deemed appropriate. In our two stories, neither man could see unemployment, even when it was not accompanied by immediate financial threat, as an opportunity to spend more time with his children or to develop sides of himself that had been forced to lay dormant because of the pressures of having to be the breadwinner. When women rise against the law of patriarchal culture, they are, indeed, on the side of men. There is a deep truth in the union song "Bread and Roses" that "the rising of the women means the rising of the race." Nelson did not feel he was worthy of his family or, indeed, that he even deserved to continue to live because he did not measure up as a man. Feminists challenge the rigid law of gender identity that sets up that measure in the first place. If fatherhood were not loaded with all the heaviness of patriarchal meaning, it could be taken up with much more joy. The fathers' movement does not even consider the possibility that it is making fatherhood terribly scary by insisting that men be *father* with a capital F. Insensitively, it turns away from tragedies such as the suicide of Nelson. The carrot of masculine domination in the family should better be understood as a killing weed, and not just for women.

Are Men Really as Bad as All That?

The fathers' movement describes men as "burdened" with such great sexual prowess that they must be tamed, that's why the carrot of male domination is necessary and why women must treat men as if they were the heads of the family. The description of men is drawn in such broad outlines that it appears as caricature. Of course, one could respond that all men are not like that. The Lacanian analysis of masculinity, however, would supply us with another analysis of the fathers' movement's description of men. The description can itself be understood as a compensatory fantasy and, more specifically, as a defensive reaction against the fear of castration. Work alone can be taming. It would be hard to run around with women and work as hard as Morris and Nelson did. The day-to-day humiliations many men have to endure at the hand of employers undermine their feeling that they are men. Better to imagine oneself as a great stud than Walter Mitty or the beaten-down Willy Loman of Arthur Miller's *Death of a Salesman*.[14] Perhaps no playwright has shown more eloquently the devastating effects on individual men of castration games played out at work than David Mamet in *Glenngarry Glen Ross*.[15]

The losers end up fired. By taking up their place in sales competitions, they put their "dick" on the line. And, as would be expected, some lose it. Those who fail in the sales competition are "fucked." The compensatory fantasy of the all-powerful stud allows one to find, in fantasy, a different image of oneself as a man. Women don't fare well in these fantasies because they now have to be the ones who get it "in the ass," showing that there is still something left of the man despite his loss at work. The fantasy does hold the promise that women should be available to make the man feel manly. Indeed, some pornographic images portray women as both the source of and the proper targets of the pent-up aggression. Women, in other words, become the displaced objects of rage for the high price the world of work demands of men. The description of men in the fathers' movement can normatively backfire, unconsciously being read as what men should be. There is then a double message in the way men are portrayed by the movement. After all, who wants to be the good family man, leaving the stud to have all the fun with all those women? The stud, man that he is, will prove himself by fighting the "draft" of marriage. It is only the wimp who will capitulate. The man's man will take his gun and go with it where he will.

EQUALITY AND LEGAL REFORM

Personhood for All

The effect of the description of men in the fathers' movement is to banish men to the realm of the phenomenal.[16] It was Immanuel

Kant who argued that as human beings, we are free to pull ourselves together. As persons, we are irreducible to our natural impulses. Although I and many others have criticized the philosophical basis of Kant's own divide among the noumenal self, the free moral person, and the phenomenal self—the creature immersed in needs and desires—we do not need to adopt his metaphysics to argue that human beings are more that just a bundle of impulses.

Much of the coercive legislation denies men their personhood, and for that reason alone it should be politically suspect. Legislation proposed by the fathers' movement also denies women their full moral standing as persons. First, measures such as cutting women off welfare use women as a means to an end, the end supposedly being that they will join the effort to round up husbands. Laws against divorce do the same for both men and women. Closing the sperm banks denies lesbian couples as well as single women access to parenthood.

Despite the many reforms of women's social standing, family law has yet to fully separate women's legal identity from the enforcement of duties in the family. Family law's continuing identification of women's legal standing with her fulfillment of certain duties in the heterosexual family is made especially evident in the treatment of lesbian parents. Scholar and activist Jacqui Alexander was banished from her country (Trinidad) for coming out as a lesbian parent.[17] Her country had passed seemingly progressive legislation to protect women in the heterosexual family; for example, laws had been passed against spousal abuse and firm civil and criminal penalties are imposed with those laws. Women are protected as wives, mothers, and as reproducers of the next generation. Despite being a mother and contributing to the reproduction of the next generation of workers, Alexander was not only ostracized but also banished outright. In the United States, lesbian parents are not banished outright, but often they are denied access to their children, as are heterosexual women who do not meet the conventional duties of wife and mother.

The State's Legitimate Interest in the Regulation of Families

In a politically liberal society, the state's legitimate interests in family regulation must be consistent with the recognition of both men and women as free and equal persons.[18] The state should have no right to privilege or impose one form of family structure or sexuality over another. This would mean that some adults could choose *consensual* polygamy. Mormon men could have more than one wife. Four women who worship the mother goddess also could recognize and form a unity and call their relationship a marriage. There would be no state-enforced single relationship—not monogamy, heterosexuality, polygamy, or polyandry.

However, it is clear that children need to have stability. How can we provide children with secure homes without institutionalizing and enforcing one form of family life? Custodial responsibility would be separated from sexual alliances. Paraparenting is already a social reality. I take seriously the concern of those who write against divorce because of the damaging effect it has on children. Say, for example, a gay man and a straight woman adopt a baby. Their parenting alliance can be broken up only due to extraordinary circumstances. If a gay couple and a lesbian couple chose to become paraparents of the child of one of the lesbian partners, the same conditions would apply. If the lesbian couple or the gay couple broke up, they would still be parents facing all the restrictions of freedom of movement that parents do now. Again, it would be due only to extraordinary circumstances that one of the parents would lose her legal status as parent. Of course, the more individuals that get involved in the paraparenting arrangement, the more potential there is for conflict. There is also more potential for child care. Many of us are informally creating these kind of extended kinship systems now. But they cannot be legalized. My argument is that they should be. We have to expect adults to realize that their sexual lives should not be allowed to completely govern the child's life. If women were completely freed from the connec-

tion of their status in the family with their duties as wives and mothers, then they would no longer be as vulnerable as they currently are under joint custody arrangements that enforce traditional heterosexuality and traditional gender roles. Do I think that people will be running to join these kinds of custodial responsibility teams in droves? Given the ontologically shattering fact of the ascension into parenthood, the answer is no.

It is understandable that the changes that have taken place in our family structure have frightened people. The political response, which alleges to legislate love and conscript men, is a sign of the fear of, not a solution to, the crisis of families. Intimate associations are different undertakings. They always have been so. The freedom to form families opens up the possibility of people creating their own families in the way most suitable to them. It opens up possibilities rather than foreclosing experimentation. If we seek to repopulate the world with lasting love, it can be only on the basis of freely formed unions.

NOTES

1. David Blankenhorn, *Fatherless America: Confronting Our Most Urgent Social Problem* (New York: Basic Books, 1995).

2. See generally David Popenoe, *Life Without Father* (New York: The Free Press, 1996); Christopher Harding, *Wingspan: Inside the Men's Movement* (New York: St. Martin's Press, 1992); and Michael L. Schwalbe, *Unlocking the Iron Cage: the Men's Movement, Gender Politics, and American Culture* (New York: Oxford University Press, 1996).

3. Nancy Chodorow, *The Reproduction of Mothering: Psychoanalysis and the Sociology of Gender* (Berkeley: University of California Press, 1978) and *Femininities, Masculinities, Sexualities: Freud and Beyond* (Lexington, KY: University of Kentucky Press, 1994).

4. Jessica Benjamin, *The Bonds of Love: Psychoanalysis, Feminism and the Problem of Domination* (New York: Pantheon Books, 1980). See also Jessica Benjamin, *Like Subjects, Love Objects: Essays on Recognition and Sexual Difference* (New Haven, CT: Yale University Press, 1995).

5. Feminists have effectively demonstrated that women lose under the imposition of the formal equality presupposed by joint custody. Due to continu-

ing economic discrimination, men often have effectively claimed that they should be given sole custody because the woman has become unstable under the strain of trying to go it alone. Often changed economic circumstances make it desirable for the woman to move to a part of the country where she can more easily survive on whatever money she can make plus child support. Yet under a joint custody arrangement, attempts at relocation can be effectively blocked. Some feminists have concluded that the reality has been so detrimental to women that we should return to the legal presumption of custody being given to the mother. Others have gone beyond that advocating that we rethink the very idea of the sexual family and the role men play in it. See Martha Fineman, *The Neutered Mother, the Sexual Family and Other Twentieth Century Tragedies* (New York: Routledge, 1995). Fineman's conclusions that male lovers should no longer be considered part of the parental family unit would be evidence for the fathers' movement that some feminists at least do want to end the role of fathers in the family. I offer an alternative feminist reform of family law that does not advocate the exclusion of male husbands and lovers from the family. See Fineman for a succinct analysis of the debate over the move to joint custody among feminists, in part 2, pp.66-87.

6. Internal membership report of the United Auto Workers on the state of the auto industry in the United States, 1995.

7. Economic Policy Institute, *The State of Working America* (Armonk, NY: M.E. Sharpe, 1990-91).

8. Carol Stack and Katherine Newman. "Finding Work in the Inner City: How Hard Is It Now?," *Russell Foundation Working Papers, 76.*

9. V.L. Burt, et al. "Trends in the Prevention, Awareness, Treatment and Control of Hypertension in Adult U.S. Populations," *Hypertension* 26 (199), 60-69.

10. See Studs Terkel, *Working* (New York: Pantheon Books, 1974).

11. I borrow this phrase from the title of Stanley Fish's book, *There's No Such Thing as Free Speech and It's a Good Thing Too* (New York: Oxford University Press, 1994).

12. See Jacques Lacan, "The Significance of the Phallus" in Juliet Mitchell and Jacqueline Rose (eds.), *Feminine Sexuality*, trans. Jacqueline Rose (London: Macmillan, 1982).

13. See Drucilla Cornell, *Beyond Accommodation* (New York: Routledge, 1991). See chap. 3, p.119.

14. Arthur Miller, *Death of a Salesman* (New York: Viking Press, 1949).

15. David Mamet, *Glengarry Glen Ross* (New York: Grove Press, 1983).

16. I borrow this phrase created by Nikol Alexander in our discussions about our essay. Cornell and Alexander, "Dismissed or Banished: A Testament to the Reasonableness of the O.J. Simpson Jury" in Toni Morrison and Claudia Schaeffer (eds.), *Birth of a Nation'hood* (New York: Pantheon Books, 1997).

17. Jacqui Alexander, "Not Any(Body) Can Be a Citizen: The Politics of Law, Sexuality and Postcoloniality in Trinidad and Tobago and the Bahamas," *Feminist Review* (Autumn 1994), n.48.

18. Cornell, *The Imaginary Domain* (New York: Routledge, 1995).

Contributors

DRUCILLA CORNELL (Professor of Law, Rutgers University Law School) is a leading international scholar in the fields of legal theory and psychoanalytic theory. She is the author of *The Imaginary Domain: A Discourse on Abortion, Pornography, and Sexual Harassment* (Routledge, 1995); *Transformations: Recollective Imagination and Sexual Difference* (Routledge, 1993); *The Philosophy of the Limit* (Routledge, 1992); and *Beyond Accommodation: Ethical Feminism, Deconstruction and the Law* (Routledge, 1991). In addition, she has co-edited four books and published over 35 articles in the field of feminist legal theory. She is also an active member of the United Auto Workers Union, with whom she was a field organizer.

CYNTHIA R. DANIELS (Associate Professor, Political Science Department, Rutgers University) is the author of *At Women's Expense: State Power and the Politics of Fetal Rights* (Harvard University Press, 1993), which won the American Political Science Association's 1993 Victoria Schuck Award for the best book in the field of women and politics. She has published numerous articles on the concept of "reproductive responsibility," motherhood, fatherhood, and fetal politics and is currently working on a book on gender and public policy entitled *Women, Citizenship and State Power,* forthcoming from Harvard University Press. Professor Daniels previously has taught at Harvard University and has been the recipient of fellowships from the Bunting Institute, the American Association of University Women, and the Woodrow Wilson Foundation.

LISA DODSON (Research Fellow, Radcliffe Public Policy Institute) has spent the last two decades researching the lives of poor women and girls in America and helping to provide health and educational services to low-income schools and neighborhoods in Massachusetts. She received her Ph.D. in Social Policy from the Florence Heller School of Social Welfare at Brandeis University and is currently principal investigator for an ethnographic research project on the impact of welfare reform on women and their families. Lisa Dodson's book, *"Don't Call Us Out of Name": The Untold Lives of Women and Girls in Poor America*, is forthcoming from Beacon Press. She was the recipient of the Alfred E. Frechette Award for outstanding achievement in public health for her work establishing the country's first comprehensive, multicultural "Women's Health Unit" through the Massachusetts Department of Public Health.

JEAN BETHKE ELSHTAIN (Professor of Social and Political Ethics, University of Chicago) is the author of over ten books, including *Rebuilding the Nest: A New Commitment to the American Family* (co-editor, Family Services Publications 1990); *Women and War* (Basic Books, 1987); *The Family in Political Thought* (University of Massachusetts, 1982); and *Public Man, Private Woman* (Princeton University Press, 1981). She is also the author of hundreds of essays in scholarly journals and journals of civic opinion, and has written some one hundred-fifteen book reviews. She has been the recipient of many awards and fellowships and has appeared regularly on national television and radio.

MAGGIE GALLAGHER is an independent scholar at the Institute for American Values and the author of *The Abolition of Marriage: How We Destroy Lasting Love* (1996). She has written widely in national newspapers and journals on questions of marriage, divorce, and family values (including the *New York Times, New Republic, The Wall Street Journal,* and *National Review*) and has appeared on National Public Television's evening *NewsHour with Jim Lehrer.*

ROBERT L. GRISWOLD (Professor of History and Women's Studies, University of Oklahoma) is the author of *Fatherhood in America: A History* (Basic Books, 1993) and *Family and Divorce in California* (State University of New York Press, 1982). He has published widely on the topic of fatherhood, parenting, and family structure in historical perspective.

SARA MCLANAHAN (Professor of Sociology and Public Affairs at Princeton University) conducts research in the areas of single parenthood, child support policy, and child well-being. She is co-author of *Single Mothers and Their Children: A New American Dilemma; Child Support Assurance: Design, Issues, Expected Impacts and Political Barriers; Child Support and Child Well-Being; Growing Up With a Single Parent: What Helps, What Hurts;* and *Social Policies for Children.* She is currently chairman of the Population Study Section for the National Institute of Health.

DAVID POPENOE (Professor of Sociology at Rutgers University) specializes in the study of family and community life in modern societies. He is the author of nine books; his latest include *Life Without Father: Compelling New Evidence that Fatherhood and Marriage are Indispensable for the Good of Children and Society* (The Free Press, 1996) and *Promises to Keep: Decline and Renewal of Marriage in America* (ed., 1996). His articles have appeared in many newspapers, magazines, and journals (including the *New York Times, Washington Post, L.A. Times, Newsweek, USA Today,* and *Fortune*) and he has been interviewed on television and radio shows such as the *Today Show* and National Public Radio's *All Things Considered.*

DOROTHY ROBERTS (Professor at Rutgers University School of Law –Newark) teaches courses on criminal law, family law, and civil liberties. She has published more than forty articles and essays in leading law reviews, scholarly journals, newspapers, and magazines, and has co-authored a casebook on constitutional law. Her most recent book is entitled *Killing the Black Body: Race, Reproduction and the Meaning of Liberty,* published by Pantheon Press.

JUDITH STACEY (Streisand Professor of Women's Studies, University of Southern California) is the author of *In the Name of the Family: Backlash Politics and Family Values* (Beacon Press, 1996); *Brave New Families: Stories of Domestic Upheaval in Late Twentieth-Century America* (Basic Books, 1990); *Patriarchy and Socialist Revolution in China* (University of California Press, 1983); and many articles in both scholarly journals and popular magazines on family structure, single motherhood, and fatherhood. She often makes appearances on national television and radio shows debating topics related to family politics.